Guruji Dr. Chandra Bhanu Satpathy: A Unique Personality

Guruji Dr. Chandra Bhanu Satpathy: A Unique Personality

Prof. Dr. Banchhanidhi Mishra

Translated by
C.R. Pattanaik

BLACK EAGLE BOOKS
Dublin, USA

BLACK EAGLE BOOKS

USA address:
7464 Wisdom Lane
Dublin, OH 43016

India address:
E/312, Trident Galaxy, Kalinga Nagar,
Bhubaneswar-751003, Odisha, India

E-mail: info@blackeaglebooks.org
Website: www.blackeaglebooks.org

First Edition in 14.01.2023

First International Edition Published by
BLACK EAGLE BOOKS, 2024

**GURUJI DR. CHANDRA BHANU SATPATHY:
A UNIQUE PERSONALITY**
by **Prof. Dr. Banchhanidhi Mishra**
Translated by **C.R. Pattanaik**

Original Copyright © **Prof. Dr. Banchhanidhi Mishra**
Translation Copyright © **C.R. Pattanaik**

All rights reserved. No part of this publication may be reproduced, stored in a retrieval system, or transmitted, in any form or by any means, electronic, mechanical, photocopying, recording or otherwise without the prior permission of the publisher.

Cover & Interior Design: Ezy's Publication

ISBN- 978-1-64560-547-8 (Paperback)
Library of Congress Control Number: 2024937465

Printed in the United States of America

A DEVOTEE'S GRATITUDE

My husband Prof. Banchhanidhi Mishra passed away unexpectedly. In due course, when I was casually looking for things in the almirah where he used to keep his things, I was in for a pleasant surprise. I found manuscripts of two books written by him. Though I had seen him many times writing something, neither did he tell, nor did I ask what exactly were they about. However, I found out that one of them was his biography and the other one was life story of Guruji Chandra Bhanu Satpathy. I was a witness to the labours he had put in to write these books – therefore they were of immense value to me. I wished them to be printed for benefit of general public. I discussed this matter with my children and they were only too happy with my suggestion.

The biography was published on first death anniversary of my husband. As regards the second book, as the book dealt with life story of Guruji and his opinion and comments, I thought it fit to obtain Guruji's permission before printing. I sent a copy of the manuscript to him and sought his permission. Guruji was himself surprised with the contents. He was all admiration for the writings and said it had many facts and which he himself had forgotten. But he did not give his consent for publication. He opined that the book should not be published during his life time i.e. while he was living.

Strangely the opinion of Guruji instead of disappointing me, made me more determined to obtain his permission. I did not want all the labours of my late husband to go waste and persisted with Guruji for his permission. Ultimately Guru conceded defeat before disciple's entreaties and the permission was granted.

On the sacred occasion of Guru Prunima Guruji inaugurated the Odia book himself.

Then the children naturally wanted the book to reach people who did not learn Odia – as many disciples of Shri Sai Baba and Guruji did not know Odia. An English translation was called for. But inspite of my approaches to several people the book would not be translated.

Then one fine day, as if by God's intervention a friend of mine informed me that Shri Chittaranjan Pattnaik has agreed to translate the book.

He happily took the responsibility and discharged it efficiently. The English version of the book could be published only because of his hard work, love and devotion. He completed the work in a very short time. Without dedicated love and devotion it could not have been done. Language fails to express my gratitude. I offer my only prayer to Shri Sai Baba and Guruji to bless him and his family.

Today, on the Diamond Jubilee birthday of Guruji, I make this small offering to Him with devotion.

Baijayanti Mishra

THE TRANSLATOR'S NOTE

I had heard the name of Guruji Shri Chandra Bhanu Satpathy since long. But I did not expect to come in contact with Guruji so suddenly and in such a way. On that auspicious morning while we were travelling in a car, my friend Shri Braja Kumar Satapathy requested me to translate this Odia book in to English. I also thought it as an instruction of Sai Baba and agreed instantly. I have come closer to Guruji Shri Chandra Bhanu Satpathy through this book only. I have not had the good luck to meet Guruji Shri Satpathy physically till today.

Now Guruji Shri Satpathy has established himself as the chief disciple of Sai Baba, like Sariputta and Swamy Vivekananda who were chief disciples of Budhadev and Rama Krushna Paramahansh respectively. But I am surprised in one aspect. Sariputta or Swamy Vivakananda were disciples during their Guru's life time. But Guruji Shri Chandra Bhanu Satpathy appeared after almost 50 years of Sai Baba's Mahasamadhi. As mentioned in this Odia book, Guruji could be able to take himself down to 100 years by reading about Sai Baba's Mahasamadhi in Shri Sai Satcharitra and could feel standing in front of Baba's holy lifeless body, what could be more surprising than this?

However, I feel myself fortunate by translating this book into English. I am extremely grateful to Shri Ashok Kumar Mohapatra, retired Asst. General Manager, SBI, who has sincerely gone through the manuscript and edited it. I am also thankful to Prof. Fakir Mohan Sahoo for his inspiration to undertake this project. I thank Sri Bijay Kumar Mohanty for his effortless DTP work. I request the readers to forgive me for any unintentional omissions or commissions.

Chitta Ranjan Pattanaik
30(P), Gajapati Nagar
Po- Sainik School
Bhubaneswar, Odisha-751005
Mob. – 9437041915 / 9937542915

- Whenever you undertake to do something, do it thoroughly or not at all.

    – Sai Baba

- Once we surrender to God completely, He will take care of us in every way.

    – Sai Baba

- There is only one caste, the caste of humanity. There is only one religion, the religion of Love. There is only one Language, the Language of heart.

    – Sai Baba

- The shortest distance between two points is a straight Line. Therefore always adhere to the straight path in life.

    – Guruji Dr. Chandra Bhanu Satpathy

- Love can not sustain without mutual tolerance, and devotion can not exist without Love.

    – Guruji Dr. Chandra Bhanu Satpathy

- The Guru is always hidden in the disciple, when the worldly covers are taken out the real image of the Guru manifests.

    – Guruji Dr. Chandra Bhanu Satpathy

CONTENTS

Prologue	13
Some informations regarding the family of Shri Chandra Bhanu Satpathy.	31
Guruji Shri Chandra Bhanu Satpathy's educational qualification and his expertise in sports	41
Various works of Guruji Shri Chandra Bhanu Satpathy.	65
The Philanthropic Programmes of Guruji	68
Helping the under privileged people	70
Contribution to Literature By Guruji Satpathy	76
The arrival of Sai Baba in Guruji Shri Chandra Bhanu Satpathy's life and other Sadgurus	87
Shri Sai Questions and Solutions	120
A bunch of messages	125
Some of the excellent Books written by Guruji Shri Chandra Bhanu Satpathy	131
"Do not fear death" – An important advice from Shri Sai Baba.	151
Shri Sai Mantra with meaning	161
Some informations about a few Sadgurus and Saints	168
Shriguru Bhagabat : Revival of Guru Tattva	173
Guruji Shri Chandra Bhanu Satpathy has expressed some of the following idealistic ideas: Those are –	186
Chanakya Niti	190
Propagation and expansion of Sai Leela in different countries	193
Some meaningful and spiritual analysis by Guruji Shri Chandra Bhanu Satpathy (Good and bad signs)	204

PROLOGUE

The prologue or introduction of a book is generally written at the end stage of the book writing. But it is placed at the beginning of the book and very few people read it. At times the size of the prologue is limited to one page only. Some writers think that it is not necessary to write prologues at all but their responsibility ceases by conveying their gratitude to them who have helped them in some way. But in my view, the prologue is the foundation of the book and it indicates what is inside the book and what is the viewpoint of the author. All the readers must go through this chapter of the book.

In this prologue, I have analysed some incidents experienced by me along with other matters. In my opinion, this analysis is essential and will help to increase the standard of the book.

I have met so many saints before I came in contact with the Sai-devotee respected Shri Chandra Bhanu Satapathy. At the time of meeting with the saints and also afterwards, I felt a sense of disillusionment with them. Perhaps it was not correct. I remember, in June 1977, the Chancellor of Berhampur University had deputed me to Goa Marine Science Research Institute. The purpose of my deputation was to study the feasibility of opening a Marine Science department in the University. If so, the requirements for it, I had to analyse in detail by visiting many Laboratories and submit a report. I reached Pune and started for Goa by another train. At that time, two or four passengers could travel in a first class cabin. There was no body except me in my cabin. But after sometime, a person wearing Silk Punjabi and white dhoti sat in front of my berth. Two persons had come up to the compartment to see him off and departed when the train left the Station. That gentleman had imparted some information on my destination Panjim and Goa, which were unknown to me earlier. I had informed him some details regarding the purpose of my travel. He did not express much after knowing that I was a Lecturer and Scientist. Generally, I do not talk much with this type of people. When I asked him regarding his occupation, he avoided it and told "you will know everything in the next Station. The next Station was Londa. Actually the station was cramped with around five hundred people. Then two or three ladies and gentlemen entered the Compartment, prostrated before this gentleman and took his attaché with them. Before descending from the train compartment, that gentleman looked at me in such a way that as if I was very insignificant in comparison to him. Many men were touching his feet on the platform. But the sight of the gentleman was on me – As though I would feel that he is high up in the ladder of this world and I am at the bottom of the ladder. The necessity of writing this experience was to apprise that many leaders, gurus (generally they are not in any occupation) are eager to show themselves off before others. There are some other persons who do not want to exhibit themselves as famous and important. I had met so many times with Guruji but they were purely family related and formal meetings. I have never met him as a professor. I met him only to discuss regarding Saibaba and Sai temple. Once, while talking, I showed off myself as a very eminent person. Though he understood everything still did not react at all. Since that day I have changed my way of talking. Perhaps, Saibaba had indirectly imposed on me to do this. Generally we used to meet whenever I went to Delhi on some work and he discussed with me on various matters for long periods.

Here I intend to remind that there are very few people who do not want to publicise their greatness. Guruji Shri Chandra Bhanu Satapathy neither desires to show off his eminence nor hear it from anybody. Even he objects if addressed as "Guruji". This type of character is seen in Walt Disney, the American animation film producer. Even, for so many days his own daughter did not know the profession or job of her father Walt Disney. Suddenly, one day the friends of the girl took her to watch a cartoon film. The friends did not realise that the maker of that cartoon film was the father of their friend. They told that the producer of this Cartoon film is world famous Walt Disney All had enjoyed the film and profusely thanked the producer. But the mind of the girl was perturbed – who is this Walt Disney? Is he her father? She returned to her house and asked her father whether he knows Walt Disney. Father enquired, which Walt Disney? The daughter explained, that Disney who has produced very good Cartoon films. Do you know him? He revealed that he knew him thoroughly and the person sitting here in front of you is Walt Disney. Immediately the daughter embraced her father and thanked him exuberantly. The reason for writing this is that the people who have reached the higher levels do not want to speak or hear regarding their greatness and importance. These types of people are very rare in the world. Shri Chandra Bhanu Satapathy is a modest, simple and helpful man. Almost all Sai devotees know it. There is no doubt regarding his contribution to the society and propagating, spreading the activities (Leelas) of Saibaba in many countries of the world. Since long time I was thinking of writing his biography but many questions aroused in my mind whether I would succeed or not. Lastly I was determined to finish this work within a few days and decided to start the work after getting permission from Shriman Satpathy. I was in doubt to get the necessary referential papers for the writing on this book. But with much difficulty I could arrange most of the materials. I prayed to Saibaba to bless me to finish this work smoothly. I was not able to view Saibaba inside the Samadhi Mandir but could catch sight of Baba from outside. May be, it was due to lack of time. This had happened in December 1995. We were compelled to return. Second time during the month of January 1997 I had the opportunity to touch the holy feet of Saibaba and also met Guruji Shri Satpathy. He talks very sweetly, at times cut jokes also but never gets angry with anybody. Here I want to advise that the anger of a man cannot solve any problem. Rather it complicates it. There is no doubt that many problems will vanish automatically if you can control your anger. Another thing, we all tend to be agitated suddenly. This creates discomposure in body and mind. You should not upset yourself if any man or some men abuse you or misbehave with you (with or without any reason). There is no doubt that you will lose your sense of thinking by your upset mind. If someone wants to play pranks while you are in a virtuous mood then you should keep calm though it is not acceptable. Good people, saintly people never care for the abuse or ill treatment meted out to them because it is true that whoever abuses others his tongue is tarnished not that of abused person's – Guruji Satpathy is in such a class of people who never bothers about intentionally motivated remarks.

Please refer to the biography of Mr. Abraham Lincoln. He was the President of United States of America. Before being President, he was working in a shop with scanty salary. As the shop was incurring losses, it could not run for long. Lincoln had availed some loan which he had repaid with interest in eighteen years. While working in that shop, he had noticed that the Negros were chained and beaten at the time of working. This sight had hunted his sentiment so much that he promised to abolish the slavery if he would get any chance in future. That also happened. He abolished this system within few months of taking oath as the President of U.S.A. The slavery had been eliminated completely but President Lincoln passed away by the bullet of a criminal, Hundreds of prostrations to that benevolent soul.

A. DISCUSSION ON ADDRESSING SHRI CHANDRA BHANU SATAPATHY AS GURUJI.

Almost all sai devotees and the persons motivated by Sai's inspiration use to address Shri Chandra Bhanu Satapathy as "Guruji". This must be started from Uttar Pradesh or Haryana. Because the persons connected with religious institutions were called as "Guruji" by the people of these States. I have gone so many times to Varanasi University as an examiner but usually they address me as professor sir. It seems that there is no relation between university or college qualifications and calling someone as "Guruji". Then how this word "Guruji" came in to existence? As per my analysis the use of this word based on his own work, not for any government or nongovernment assignments. His work was to evaluate the horoscopes and accordingly predicting the future of the person concerned, matching the horoscopes, how the pyramid is related to the health of the general people and the influence of different weeds on the health of a patient etc. etc. These activities are not included in his police service. Here I am imparting a little information which I have heard from many people on this matter. The marriage of a thirty year old girl could not be materialized. When they had approached Guruji Satpathy babu, he instructed them that the marriage of the girl could take place if she could carry a sack of coal on her back and shoulder and throw it in river water. The girl did not agree to it at all. But after much persuasion, the coal sack was touched to the back and shoulder of the girl and thrown in to the Mahanadi water. After three months of this incident of sack throwing, a marriage proposal was initiated and the marriage of that girl was settled with a gentle and high officer and the marriage was completed without any hassle.

Another story – There was a meeting in Swosti Premium Hotel. Guruji Satpathy was the Chief Guest of that meeting and he has to deliver a speech on that occasion. Many people come to consult with Guruji regarding the Sai temples in their respective places. I was also present in that gathering. My wife, daughter and son-in-law had also accompanied me. The speech of Guruji was precise and meaningful.

After that Shri J.K. Mohanty, the owner or the Swosti Hotel, spoke something on Guruji. What he had narrated is given below.

The construction work of the hotel did not progress despite the land for it was already demarcated. The government had also permitted to construct the hotel on that govt. land but no development took place at all. Mohanty babu informed everything to Guruji Shri Satpathy over telephone. He advised that a piece of leather was lying somewhere in the land. Throw it outside and the work would be finished smoothly. Actually a piece of leather was found inside the land and only after that bit of leather was thrown out, the work of the hotel building commenced and finished in time. The Chief Minister of Odisha was invited to inaugurate the hotel. In the last moment, it was detected that the air conditioning system of the hotel was not working. It was difficult to call the French Company for the repair. No doubt it would take at least one on two days. In a last resort, Mohanty babu informed the matter to Guruji over phone. He instructed to put two or three sacks of wheat on the roof top of the hotel. In this situation, anybody could think it as a joke but there was no other way. At last as per the instruction of the Guruji, they had kept two sacks of wheat on the roof top. Wonder of wonders, the air conditioning system started functioning after a few moments of keeping these sacks on the roof top. Nobody understands the relation between wheat sacks and the air conditioning. Apart from it, I have heard from others many such incidents performed by respected Shri Satpathy.

Perhaps he is called "Guruji" due to the above reasons.

THE MEETING OF THE AUTHOR WITH GURUJI AND TOUCHING THE FEET OF SADGURU SAIBABA

In January 1997, I and my wife decided to visit Siridi from Mumbai. One of my students at Jeypore College, Sriman Amiya Sahu, an owner of a small mechanical factory, had arranged a car for our journey to Shiridi and requested us to return after a day or one & half days. Again that gentleman told us in the night that tomorrow morning Mr. Arup Pattanaik with his family and Capt. Panda would go to Shiridi and they would pick up us from our place. I had asked why the program changed suddenly. He clarified that, Guruji has come to Shridi and he will stay there for two days. We, all are going to meet him. I met Guruji for the first time in Shiridi. Before that, I did not know anything about him. Afterwards, I came to know that he is the younger brother of one of my students. (Mitrabhanu Satpathy).

HERE I AM WRITING A LITTLE REGARDING THE PRAYER WHICH IS HIGHLY ESSENTIAL FOR ALL SAI DEVOTEES

Perhaps to say a prayer may not be in daily or weekly agenda but it is a step to move forward towards the Omniscient God. Many people express that they have no time to pray. But they constantly continue to gather wealth and forget the Almighty. They run to temples, churches or masjids to worship only at the time of their bad period. When asked regarding their prayer, they explained that they faced many difficulties in further accumulating wealth and the accumulated riches with them were reducing day by day. Amassing property is a mental disease. Once a very big rich man went to Guru Nanak and said that his earning of money is not increasing rather reducing to some extent. After hearing everything thoroughly Guru Nanak gave a needle to the gentleman and told him to return it to him in the other world. That rich man did not understand the inner meaning of this and handed over that needle to his wife with a request to keep it carefully, because he has to return it to Guru Nanak in the next world. As she was a wise lady, she understood the meaning and asked her husband, can we carry this needle after our death ? Can any material things will accompany us? The true purpose of this story is that, whatever we are earning (by legal or illegal means) will stay behind this world. Only our benevolent deeds will accompany you.

Another example is regarding our worship or offering arati which is done only for the fulfillment of some essential necessities like daughter's marriage, suffering from severe disease, no money to purchase a car, to get a good house etc. etc. They blame the God if their needs are not fulfilled. I know from my own experience that some persons (they pose themselves as devotees) hold their revered Gods and goddesses responsible for their pathetic condition. Someone uses to tell "I have done so many pujas but without any result; now I have no loyalty towards Baba". I had inquired - had you come to Baba when you are in affluent condition? The answer was a clear "No". The essences on these things are that, we, by any chance, do not remember the God at our happier times and our alibi is lack of time. When our bad period arrives, we usually tend to pray to our gods and goddesses. Prayer should be done regularly and as per routine. Perhaps for this the aratis of Saibaba are performed perfectly four times in a day. This can be called routine as generally there is no change in the timing of aratis. If there is at all any change, then it is determined by the timing of sunrise and sunset.

THE SAI CURRENT

What is Sai Current? The philosophy of Sai baba's life has been described abundantly in many books along with Sai Satcharitra. By reading these, the readers not only acquire knowledge but also surely feel exhilarated due to this Sai current, no doubt about it. The three levels of Baba's life are presented in this book. The centre of the Sai Current is "eternity" and Sai Baba is infinite and omnipresent. As per Sai Satcharitra, He exists before and after the creation of this universe. By going through different stages of evolution, he appeared on this planet as an incarnation of goodness with absolute powers.

Guruji Shriman Chandra Bhanu Satpathy explained in detail the principle of Guru and the principle of Avatar in his books "Gopya ru Agopya" and "Shree Guru Bhagabat". Three directions are observed in this current.

1. Emergence of Abatari Person
2. Supernatural events
3. Equality of all religions

Many Sai Current events relating to divine thoughts are described in the book "Chirantan Sai Prabaha" of Sriman Amulyaratna Nanda. Like Shri Sainath other preachers (Budhadeb, Jishuchrista, Mohammed and Adishankar) also jump into this bio-ocean – considering different angles of the Sai Current, Sriman Nanda has divided time into different periods which are given below.

(A) 1854 to 1858 – Appearance of Sai Baba. Of course, his birth and childhood activities are still a mystery.

(B) 1859 to 1886 - Due to spiritual flow during this time, Sai Baba has been described as a poor Fakir with special powers. In the year 1886 Baba had left his Physical body for three days.

(C) 1887 to 1909 – The penniless Sainath was transformed to Sainath Maharaj and Sainath Sadguru during this period.

(D) 1910 to 1918 – The Sai current flowed with tremendous momentum.

(E) 1919 to 1930 – The speed of Sai current slowed down

to some extent. But different magazines relating to Sai activities were published and the Shiridi Sai Sansthan was formed.

1931 to 1960 – The role of Narasingh Swamy in research of Sai Baba's life and writing on Sai Baba and special efforts of devotees in spreading Sai activities are worthy of attention.

1961 to 1990 – Many books and magazines in different languages (Hindi, English and Telgu) on numerous plays (Leelas) or Sai Baba were published.

From 1990 to date, the promotion and propagation of Shiridi Sai Baba's philosophy has been increased many fold in our country as well as foreign countries. Many Sai temples and Sai Centres have been established in different places. The Sai devotees are trying with determination for the spreading and publicizing the Sai philosophy during this Sai Current.

In this process, the role of Shri Chandra Bhanu Satpathy is a special and sincere effort. He came in contact with Sai Baba in 1989 and the power of Sai current had touched him for the first time. Under his responsibility hundreds of Sai temples and Sai information Centers were setup in our country and foreign countries also. In his direction, the construction work of hundreds of Sai temples and different Sai institutions are going on even now. Guruji has advised to all Sai devotees and Sai followers through some of his quality writings and messages on Sai doctrine. The temples were constructed for a special purpose. Has any attention been given for it? Some temples are developing continuously like an infant develops to a youth. All Sai devotees should remember that development does not mean

to deviate from the noble cause. He has further advised that the following five works are not acceptable to him.
1. To worship his photo
2. To touch his feet or Prostrate before him.
3. To praise or appreciate
4. To pray only for personal problems.
5. To accept his left-overs as Prasad.

(Sai Vani – 2003 October 25 – Diwali issue).

I also request all Sai devotees not to perform the above mentioned activities. I hope and request again that they should convey this matter to their friends. Sai current is a supernatural phenomenon and the events happen here are no doubt natural. A lot of books are written on Baba's life and philosophy comparing with Sufi and Nath Community. On many instances books are written, songs are composed on Baba comparing him with Sri Bishnu, Hanuman and Ganesh. But in my opinion, Baba's philosophy cannot be compared with any one particular doctrine. From his lifestyle nobody can identify him as Hindu or Muslim. The life and ideal of Baba can be judged from the point of view of the public and can be compared with Bhagabat Geeta which is tested several times by the touch stone of time.

Amulya babu had faced many complicated circumstances to write the book "Sai Prabha". First critical situation was his health condition, second was to get different books or magazines on Baba where many playful activities (Leelas) of Baba are presented. Those were available due to the help of Guruji and Nanda babu succeeded in his effort. The specialty of this book is that it is pretty easy to understand the life of Baba, the Sadguru.

All Sai followers should read the book "Chintan Sai Prabah" written by Sriman Amulya Ratna Nanda. Here he has written the creative plays (Leelas) of Baba during the period from 1854 to 1918 for the knowledge of all Sai disciples. On 25th October 2003 (Diwali) Shri Chandra Bhanu Satpathy had sent messages to many Sai devotees in Delhi describing how to self-manage in sai path and enhance the spiritual knowledge. He had written in the message to think why and how they met? Was it not for the sake of Baba? Has not Baba helped us in every level ? Are we paying proper attention to the purpose for which the temples were built? After analysing the above factors, please concentrate how to manage smoothly and efficiently as per the direction of Sai path.

THE PRESENTATION OF GURUJI CHANDRA BHANU SATPATHY ON THE DOCTRINE OF BIRTH AND DEATH CYCLE AND SALVATION FROM IT

Birth and death are the two irrevocable Laws or human life. There is no dispute that after birth, death is inevitable. No animal can avoid the principle of birth and death circle. Single cell animals and plants are also included in this Law. The most astonishing factor is that the animals / plants existing since lakhs of years still remain unknown. Their life history, size, movements and activities are secret to us even now. The scientists are continuing their research on these creatures.

What happens when an animal leaves its body and after it? Is there any existence of soul power? Can this soul power influence the next life? As per Hindu religion an animal has to take birth again and again. There is possibility of getting salvation after many births. In Buddhism this salvation is called "Nirvana". In Hinduism the saints have instructed to restrain from doing any bad activities since childhood and always try to do benevolent deeds. The Hindus believe that every action has its equal consequences which prove Newton's Law of "for every action there is an equal and opposite reaction". One has to endure the consequences of his previous actions. But this endurance may not be completed in one birth but extended to many births. The truth to this maxim is proved in many Hindu scriptures.

Different ways are instructed in Hindu religion to get salvation from this painful circle of birth and death. Accordingly some built temples, some offer food to the hungry and some visit the sacred places but these acts with motive are against the principle of Hinduism. Further, Guruji writes that there is no end to the rebirth if one has a desire rather it will delay his birth circle. Therefore, only selfless work controls the birth circle. This rebirth is mentioned in "Shri Sai Satcharitra" and other books relating to Sai Baba. Baba had divulged to some of his devotees regarding their previous births.

He has advised to lead the life patiently, tolerantly and with sacrifice with unlimited faith on God. Baba has not said anything on "heaven". Keep your mind pure, stay away from negative thoughts, do some good acts to others, pray to the God. Those were some of the advices of Sai Baba.

Please ask a question to Baba if you have any doubt in your mind. Definitely, Baba will answer if the question is asked honestly from the inner core of your heart. It is no doubt true.

CONCENTRATION - AN IMPORTANT ADVICE OF SAI BABA

Concentration is a psychological necessity of human beings. If we will do some work without concentration then some mistakes will take place or some disturbances may occur and the works have to be started once again from the beginning. Generally barbers, blacksmiths, carpenters, weavers and different other professionals are established in the society through their successive generations. They all are concentrating in their respective occupations. If a blacksmith, at the time of striking the red hot iron or melting the iron in fire, loses his concentration even for a few seconds, then something wrong happens and his work remains incomplete. This statement is absolutely true. Only with the attentiveness, blacksmith is able to manage his work efficiently. Like that, if a barber unmindfully shaves by his shavette then there is every possibility of wound. Likewise the attentiveness of a goldsmith enables him to create beautiful designed ornaments. At times there are many disturbances in the house due to lack of understanding and attention. No body from the above mentioned persons have practiced concentration by reading books or going to schools or colleges. Their activity and concentration are complementary to each other. Generally, they are exposed to danger due to lack of attentiveness. This fear compels them to stay in alertness. By this their mind also remains stable – Guruji Shri Satpathy has expressed that while doing a work only concentration can complete it easily and smoothly. All the books he has written are the result of this concentration. My request to all Sai devotees is that they should do any work with full concentration. No doubt they will get good results by doing this. Here I want to tell one thing that the concentration is not limited to one generation. This is transferred from one generation to another. There is no need to go to any school for this. At times those are engaged in family trade can learn easily in a laboratory. Perhaps this genealogical concentration has helped them to complete their task perfectly. If the son of a blacksmith has been admitted to I.T.I., then he will learn the working procedure of the machines earlier than others. This is possible due to his internal qualities.

Bhagaban SriKrishna has told Arjun that "The success is derived by repeated practice, without this the mind is always fickle and unstable. This is also powerful and running till infinite time." SriKrishna said – Generally the brain of the human being and its thought process is indisciplined but to rein it, the mind should be controlled first. It is our duty to block its speedy movements. But this task is not so easy because to control it is not only difficult but also irrational. Here I want to apprise you that, the five senses (eye, ear, nose, tongue and touch) are very agile. Concentration is essentially necessary to restrain them.

A piece of paper does not catch fire if the sun rays fall on it. But if these rays pass through a double convex lens and fall on any side of the paper then the paper ignites. It was possible because all the rays of the light compressed and fell on a single point. Exactly like this, the scattered mind should be organized to be together. As per the opinion of Swamy Purushottamanandaji, one can be triumphant in any assignment if he will work with full attentiveness. No doubt about it. The same types of advice of Sai Baba are also seen in various magazines.

Sai Baba has discussed a lot on concentration at many places. In the book "Sri Sai Satcharitra" Baba himself has apprised that the human being is the best among the eighty four lakhs animals in this world. The man can able to lead a life of highest standard and also he is the finest creature amid the animal world. Yet, he is trying to immerse himself in the sin of power, pride, selfishness and ignorance. Nothing unusual in it. The nature of the man is to belittle others. This character is so dangerous that it can influence the environment of the entire world. Today our planet is moving towards destruction. Therefore, my prayer to Sai Baba is that our beautiful earth, created by the Almighty, do not fall in to the face of destruction.

GURUJI HONOURED IN FOREIGN COUNTRIES

On the occasion of first Indo-US Trade Summit, Guriji Dr. Chandra Bhanu Satpathy had been conferred with prestigious "Building the Bridges across the nations" award for his remarkable contribution in the field of art, culture, music, literature and above all humanity. In a grand ceremony held in the city of Seattle, U.S.A., Guruji had been bestowed with this prestigious honour. This was the first instance where an Odia or an Indian received such an award in America. At first the citizens of Seattle had formally expressed their gratitude for spreading the humanism through the teachings of Sadguru Siridi Sai Baba, continuously in the world with the aid of love, kindness, tolerance and purity. After the announcement made by the Mayor of Seattle City, Lieutenant Governor Brad Owen had said that the splendid works performed in present times were of great importance. The humanism of Guruji seemed utmost useful when the hatred, enmity and violence were escalating ceaselessly among the humans. He had hoped that Guruji would work towards delivering the Sai movement in every nook and corner of America. Mr. N. Parthasarathi from Indian embassy and Mr. Brad Owen, the Lieutenant Governor of Washington state had taken part in the function as esteemed guest and Chief Guest respectively. Shri Parthasarathi had congratulated Guruji for this honour and observed that the activities implemented by him for the welfare of human society is many times more than this award. There were some dance programmes enacted by the artists of India and other countries at the end of the function. While receiving the award, Guruji emphasized on using the culture, education and the need of the people to build the bridges of compassion, thereby reducing the distance between the countries. He further stated that except fulfilling the basic necessities and keeping in mind the happiness of the people, such planning and policy should be implemented by which maximum people will get opportunity to be maximum happy for the maximum period. He expressed his gratitude to the organisers for honouring him on account of the influence of Sai Baba on his life. Many senior officials from different States of India were present in this event. Governor of Washington State Mr. Kristen Gregory, Secretary Hillary Clinton, the Asia America Commercial Officer of Whitehouse Mrs. Kiran Ahuja and others had sent messages wishing success of the function.

GRATITUDE

I compliment sincerely from my heart to those who have helped me in shaping this book. I am expressing my gratitude to Prof. Bishnu Charan Chaudhury for narrating a brief account on the writer. I thank those who have helped me in writing this book (mainly Dr. Sachidananda Padhy) and others. I convey my special thanks to Smt. Debasmita and Rama Prasad.

I express my heartful gratitude to the President, treasurer of Berhampur Siridi Sai temple and Smt. Suneeta Tripathy for helping me in writing this book.

Prof. Banchhanidhi Mishra

SOME INFORMATION REGARDING THE FAMILY OF SHRI CHANDRA BHANU SATPATHY

The father of Guruji, Sri Gokul Chandra Satpathy had spent twenty five years or more in the education department of Odisha. Guruji is the second son of Gokul babu. First son, Dr. Mitrabhanu Satpathy, was one of my students in Botany department of Revenshaw College.

I did not have the opportunity to know Guruji Shriman Chandra Bhanu Satpathy when I was in Revenshaw College. Because I was not there when he was admitted in Revenshaw to study. Apart from it, relationships with many persons were interpted due to my frequent transfers during those two-year-period (i.e. from 1966 to 1968). I was at Jeypore for a few days and again went to Keonjhar in 1967, thus remained away from Revenshaw. I was away from Revenshaw after my departure to Keonjhar and Sambalpur.

A BRIEF SUMMARY ON THE FATHER OF SRIMAN SATPATHY

It seems from his many writings that Shri Chandra Bhanu Satpathy had loved his father very much. The 25th death anniversary of his father was observed on 2nd

November 2007. A souvenir was unveiled on that day in which the writings of the family members of Gokul babu and some other respected persons were published. I am writing below, in short, the versions of Guruji Shri Satpathy on his father. "In the year 1982 when he was Senior S.P. in Ajamgarh district, he got a message regarding the seriousness of his father's health. He was suffering from blood cancer and admitted in SCB Medical, Cuttack. At that time the treatment of cancer was not developed like today. Anyhow, all types of approved medicines for cancer treatment were administered on him. Despite all types of treatment, his earthly body passed away. This day was 2nd November 1982. His mortal body was brought to Baripada for cremation. It was difficult to describe the agony, mother had gone through. Mother had married at the age of eight only and lived with father for almost fifty two years. She never expected that her husband would pass away so soon. But who can obstruct the statute of Almighty."

Shriman Gokul Chandra Satpathy was a self-made person. He was able to complete his study by getting scholarship for the entire period. He had stayed almost four years (1934 to 1939) in London as the tutor of Princes of Mayurbhanj. He had lost the chance of taking his wife to London due to the outbreak of Second World War. He also obtained his B.A. (Hons) degree in English literature from London University. He had to remain in Mayurbhanj due to Second World War. In 1944 he joined Utkal University as registrar. Then he entered into the Government job. First he was School Inspector, then deputy Secretary and finally he was appointed as D.P.I. of Schools in Odisha. He was retired in 1968. He had worked as the Commissioner of Indian Scouts and Guides organization till his death. Guruji Satpathy talks a lot regarding his father. His father had reached the top-most position in the education department of Government of Odisha though born in an uncharted village in an unfamiliar family. He had helped the poor students to his level best. He knew that at that time so many students had taken pain and faced difficulties to continue their studies. This group never shows their arrogance. Here the grand father of the author is Pandit Lingaraj Mishra who had hailed from a small village. It is heart touching to describe the pains he had suffered to study in places like Puri, Varanasi etc. Perhaps we can not understand now the situation prevailed at that time for continuation of education. His demise had taken place in the early part of 1972. The purpose of writing this is that he could have adopted the occupation of priest like his other brothers. But he did not, because his aim was completely different – to acquire knowledge. It is beyond my imagination, how one could get "byakaranacharya" in an educational institution and B.O.L. along with it. His English writing was also very good. He used to correct my English too. He is no more but I will treasure his memories in my heart always. This is my only prayer to Sai Baba. He was retired from Samant Chandra Sekhar College as an efficient Lecturer in 1957. It will not be exaggerated if I state that I learnt Odia writing from him.

Guruji used to say that father may not be in his mortal body, but he is always alive in his heart and mind and remain there in future also. The elder brother of Guruji Sri Mitrabhanu Satpathy has recounted regarding his father as follows –

His father devoted himself to open many schools and educational institutions in Odisha. Many schools and educational institutions were opened in distant and remote places during his time. Not only he helped in opening them but also assisted them in the management and at times he himself arrived there for solving their problems. All the brothers, sisters, brothers-in-law of Guruji had felt the emptiness of Late Gokul Chandra Satpathy and recorded their experience in the Souvenir on his 25th death anniversary. This souvenir has kept Gokul babu alive and will keep so in future, no doubt about it.

His nephew Sri Jatindra Mohan Satpathy had divulged about Gokul babu that after two days of his retirement, his uncle had asked him to bring a lot of money order forms. After bringing them, he directed me to write the addresses on them. All the addresses were noted in a notebook. His order was to write his address as well as the addresses of the receivers in excellent hand writing. He had instructed to write on the money order forms requesting the receivers to inform him the amount of expenses incurred by him during his last inspection of that area. As per his wishes monies were deposited in the post office after filling up the money order forms. He had intimated the receivers as under.

Dear _____ babu,

My blessings to you. Many thanks for arranging my inspection. You had declined to receive the amount expended for it. From that day I was a debtor to you. Now I am feeling extremely good by repaying your debt. Hope you will accept it happily. Stay well and happily with family.

Yours

Gokul Chandra Satpathy

I was directed to fill up this type of letters in 30/40

money order forms. This process had continued for 3/4 days. His nephew Sri Jatinandra Mohan Satpathy (Retired Head Master) has written that "The money order incident is remembered by me forever".

Srijukta Jagannath Mishra, ex-head master of Secondary Board School had stated that "I have heard English language from so many persons, but nobody can speak the Simple English like Gokul Saheb."

Another incident had happened at the time of Kuamir Middle English School inspection. Leaving the vehicle at a distance, Gokul babu went out to visit the school. The Head Master Sri Chandra Mohan Panda had requested Gokul babu to take a seat but he hesitated to sit in front of his teacher. He had inspected the classes politely and said "Sir, it is impudence on my part to inspect the school before you". Very few people have such type of devotion towards their teachers. It is astonishing to hear this kind of devotion to his former teacher by England returnee Shri Gokul Chandra Satpathy.

WHAT GURUJI TELLS ABOUT HIS FATHER

Shri Gokul Chandra Satpathy, the father of Guruji, was born on 7th October 1911 in Pruthanathpur village coming under Badasahi Tahasil of Mayurbhanj. He was the second child of father Sri Sudarsan Satpathy and mother Satyabhama Satpathy. His elder brother Srinath Satpathy was ten years older than him. Pruthanathpur Brahmin Sashan is the intermediate village of Manitri and Badasahi villages. At that time, Mayurbhanj was ruled by the King of Mayurbhanj and its capital was Baripada. Now it is the district head quarters. His father passed away when he was only four-year-old and the entire burden of the family rested on mother and to some extent with his elder brother. As per family tradition, the Satpathy households were famous as Learned priests (Purohit Pandit). Apart from it, they were doing some farming. After demise of his father, their family was struggling for some days.

In his childhood, he had gone to his maternal uncle's house at Madhupur near Badasahi to continue his study and read there in Middle English school. Daily he had to walk for five miles to reach the school. Due to his sharp intelligence, he stood first in the primary examination of Mayurbhanj State in 1920 and there by drew the attention of the king of Mayurbhanj. At that time there was only one high school in Mahurbhanj. Maharaja Krushna Chandra Bhanjadeo had arranged a student scholarship of seven rupees per month to Gokul Chandra.

Before 1st April 1936, Bihar and Odisha were ruled like a joint state. At that point of time the matriculation examination of the two states were held together. He had successfully passed this jointly managed matriculation examination in 1931 and secured 2nd position in both states and first in Odisha. This exceptional achievement had glorified his school as well as the Mayurbhanj state. The respected Maharaja of Mayurbhanj, Sri Pratap Chandra Bhanjdeo had ordered a monthly scholarship of twenty five rupees for his higher education. He had passed his graduation with English honours from Revenshaw College. During the British rule, exclusive appreciation was accorded to the students of English honours. After that he had moved to Patna University to complete his post graduation in English with L.L.B. But the turning point of his life had taken a different direction there. Maharaja Shri Pratap Chandra Bhanjdeo had requested him to take care of his two sons, Pradeep Chandra and Swarup Chandra, studying at London and continue his own studies there along with it. So he travelled to London in the early part of 1936. For the Indian students, there was a rule at that time, that they have to pass the graduation degree again from their university to enable them to accomplish their post-graduation Course. Therefore, he again successfully obtained his bachelor's degree with English honours from the University College of London in the year 1938 and joined higher education. Then he was engaged, for some time, as an English teacher in a school situated at Hertfordshire in South London.

Before leaving for London for the purpose of his higher education, Shri Satpathy married Harsamayee, the daughter of Sridhar Dash and Tilottama Dash. It was a matter of great sorrow that his mother expired before his return to India. He had come back to India in 1939 to take his wife with him. His wife, Harsamayee, had stayed in hostel and passed matriculation from Revenshaw girls' High School, Cuttack. But God's wishes were different. Just at that time the 2nd world war started. (I have her passport and ship ticket with me till now). They could not travel to London anymore. In the year 1940, at the request of Keonjhar Maharaja, he proceeded to Keonjhar and took responsibility of teaching his son Nrusingh Narayan Singhdeo and daughter Swarna Prabha. During this period, his elder daughter Niyati and second daughter Bharati were born. In the year 1942, he started his career as the education Superintendent of Mayurbhanj state. He used to visit tribal dominated remote areas by motorcycle. He was planning to spread the light of education in these areas and also trying for proper implementation of these plans. His first son Mitrabhanu was born at this time. The Utkal University

Act was effective from 2nd August 1943. Shri Satpathy was selected as the first Odia Registrar of Utkal University in 1944. The then Governor of Odisha Mr. Kailashnath Katju and Dr. Prana Krushna Parija were the chancellor and vice-chancellor of the Utkal University respectively. During this time (at Cuttack residence) his sons Chandra Bhanu and Santanu had taken birth. He had worked for some time as the Secretary of Cuttack Rotary Club during this period.

In 1947, alter independence of the country, he joined as Circle Inspector of Southern division in education department. This office was situated at Berhampur. The responsibility of all the schools in all the districts and training schools of the circle was assigned to him, while at Berhampur his daughter Minati and son Diptabhanu were brought in to this world.

In the year 1955, he was promoted as deputy director of education department and was transferred to Cuttack. At that time, Dr. Balabhadra Prasad was the education director of Odisha. In 1959, he was appointed as Joint Secretary of education department in Odisha government secretariat and came to Bhubaneswar. Again in 1961, he was promoted as joint director of education department and returned to Cuttack. Towards the end of 1966, two director posts were created for higher education division and school division. Shri Satpathy had got the opportunity to work as the first director of schools division. Along with it, he was the ex-officio Chairman of board of secondary education, Odisha. He was functioning as the honourary Commissioner of Odisha Scouts and Guides till his death. He was honoured with "white elephant" award posthumously on account of his honest, unwavering and long time service to the Scout / Guide organization.

He had exceptional proficiency in three Languages (i.e. English, Odia and Sanskrit). He was contributing regularly to the then established magazines like Bhanja Pradip, Sahakar, Naba Bharat and others. He has authored a lot of high standard critical articles on medieval period of English and Odia Literature. He dedicated himself for literature till the end of his life. He was the source of inspiration to the young writers. After retirement, he was actively involved in the cultural and literary institutions of Baripada. He had built up a huge Library by collecting many books and magazine in English, Odia, Hindi, Bengli and other Languages. In the year 1976, he was felicitated by "Utkal Sahitya Samaj" and "Odisha Sahitya Akademi" for his high standard writing.

Basically he was a teacher and educationist. Many educational institutions and teacher training centres were established in Odisha by his sincere efforts. He laboured hard for the development of women's education in Odisha and to set up an university in north Odisha. The tradition of pulling the chariots only by Ladies at Baripada car festival was originally initiated by him. He was a farsighted thinker. His contribution towards reformative activities will be remembered for a long time.

Personally speaking, he was not only my father but also my teacher. I have learnt English, Odia and Sanskrit Languages from him. He had encouraged me to read the books on Odia Language. We both together, were reading Odia, English and Bengli poems. He had taught us, all the brothers and sisters, many arts like playing tabla, harmonium, singing songs, playing cards, carom and climbing trees by appointing a music teacher. He was personally giving attention to the studies of all the children.

All children had learnt Odia, English and Sanskrit from him. Whatever I am today, that is only for my father. Because, my father was the ideal or my life. Therefore, every day I remember him and crave for his blessings in my mind.

GURUJI SHRI CHANDRA BHANU SATPATHY'S EDUCATIONAL QUALIFICATIONS AND HIS EXPERTISE IN SPORTS

Shri Chandra Bhanu Satpathy has begun his school education in Ravenshaw Collegiate School, Cuttack and passed his matriculation from Pyari Mohan Academy, Cuttack. While I was reading, Utkal University was conducting the matriculation examination. After some years the examination was managed by Orissa Council of Secondary education. The old students Association of Ravenshaw Collegiate School had facilitated Shri Chandra Bhanu Satpathy as "Pride of the alumni" on 23rd January 2009. This honour was accorded to him for his contribution in the field of national and international services, literature, music, social services and spiritually motivated activities.

He had completed B.A. Honours in Political Science in 1968 from Ravenshaw College, Cuttack; affiliated to Utkal University. I was already transferred to another college at that time. The ten years (1958 to 1968) of Lectureship in Ravenshaw was the best period in my life. While studying in the college, Shri Satpathy had shown his expertise in different fields. He was the captain of College Badmiton team Apart from it , he was also adorned the post of

Secretary of Political Science Association. His eloquence in arguing in English and Odia was praise-worthy. He had represented Ravenshaw College in inter-college competitions and was also rewarded many times. Humorous and satire articles in Odia were written by him too. These articles were published in the magazines like Dagar, Asanta Kali, Jhankar and Ravenshaw College magazines.

Shriman Satpathy has successfully passed M.A. in Political Science in 1970 from Ramjas College, Delhi. While continuing his study in Delhi University; he was recognised as a formal debater of high standard in English. He was also the captain of Delhi University Badminton team.

During 1992 to 1993, while he was in Police (I.P.S) Service, he had carried out higher research on Advanced Professional Programme in Public Administration. This programme is managed by Govt. of India, New Delhi. The department of State administration, Govt. of India, New Delhi had honoured him by awarding diploma in M.Phil. The topic of his M.Phil thesis was "Indian Civil Aviation Safety - A Critical Analysis." This thesis was highly appreciated by the Punjab University. In 1993, Punjab University had given Masters Diploma (NDPA) on this thesis.

In the year 1970, Shrijukta Satpathy had joined as a Lecturer in Political Science in Hastinapur College (East Delhi). Later, this college was renamed as Motital Nehru College. He continued to work in this college up to the middle of 1972.

PROFESSIONAL CAREER – A SHORT NOTE

Shri Chandra Bhanu Satpathy was selected in Indian Police Service (I.P.S.) by Union Public Service Commission (UPSC) in the year 1972. That year he joined in Uttar Pradesh cadre.

VARIOUS EXPERIENCES IN WORKING LIFE

1. In August 1981, the President of India had conferred him with "Distinguished Police Medal" for his extreme courage. This medal was given to him for showing exceptional bravery by putting his own life in danger.

2. In 1985, while he was the Senior Superintendent of Police in Meerut, the Governor of U.P. (Lat Saheb) had awarded him a special medal for the public service done by the police force.

3. In 1991, the President of India had accorded him "President's Police Medal" for his distinguished service.

4. Again in 1997, the President of India had given him the medal on his significant and praiseworthy services.

He had worked as A.S.P. in Meerut and Aligarh for a year i.e. in 1975 to 1976. Then from 1976 to 1978 he had functioned as Additional S.P. at Moradabad. He joined as S.P. (C.I.D.) at Kanpur in 1980-81. He also worked as S.P. in Gajipur and then as senior S.P. at Ajamgarh (1981 to 1983). Again he joined as a senior S.P. at Gorakpur (1983-84) and Meerut (1984-86). These two very sensitive districts were infamous for communal violence and different crimes. Though these two districts were very sensitive still he was able to establish peace.

In 1981, when he was S.S.P. of Ajamgarh, he fought with two armed criminals inside the Ajamgarh district court premises in broad daylight and was able to save two advocates. For this he had to endure physical wound. The President of India had given him "Vishisht Police Medal" for this courageous action (by risking his own like).

In 1985, when he was S.S.P. on Meerut, the Governor of U.P had rewarded him for the excellent Public Services done by the Police force.

1986-1990 – During this period, he joined as deputy director of newly created Civil Aviation Authority of Govt. of India. This department was under the Ministry of Civil Aviation. This department was established in 1985 after Air India's Kaniska crashed to pieces in the air. Shriman Satpathy was the first police officer who was responsible for the creation of this department. Later this department was named as Bureau of Civil Aviation Security. After some days of creation of this department, he was promoted as the Additional Commissioner of the Bureau (1988). He also got promotion as the Commissioner of the Bureau in 1990. In 1991, he received Police Medal from the President of India for his excellent contribution and lifelong police service. He attended a Civil Aviation Security Seminar in London, representing India, while he was in civil aviation service (1986). In 1990, he participated in a conference on civil aviation management in Tokyo, Japan on behalf of civil aviation department of India. In January - February 1990, Shriman Satpathy, as the chief of Indian Contingent, had taken part in the convention organised by the Japan international Co-operative Agency (JICA). He also acted as the chief of the meeting in some occasions.

In 1990, he had participated in a conference relating

to international civil aviation for seven weeks in Jakarta (Indonesia). The well thought article on international civil aviation (i.e. safe civil travel, Secure Courier Service etc.) presented by him in this symposium was highly appreciated by the delegates of other countries. The international air traffic control association had especially accepted his article. He was also able to patronise the international seminar.

After the end of his deputation period in Govt. of India, he had joined at Moradabad as Inspector General of "Pradesh armed Constabulary" (PAC) in western zone. There were around 23,000 armed police in this zone which includes officer ranking Police also. Some staffs of this battalion were posted in sensitive states like Asam, Delhi and Punjab.

Honourable President had awarded him with Police medal in the year 1997 for his famous work style.

In the year 1996, the Govt. of India (Home Ministry) had selected him to attend an international Conference in Havana (Cuba), when he was posted at Provincial Armed Constabulary. Dr. Satpathy has prepared an article on penal sciences in the international conference held in Cuba. In Havana, he had delivered his speech on the system of Criminal Law in India.

1998-2003 – Dr. Satpathy was placed in New Delhi corporate office of Indian Oil Corporation as Chief Vigilance Officer (CVO). The oil corporation was able to get the ISO-9002 certificate due to his Leadership and use of some new processes. Generally this certificate (ISO) is given by the Govt. to any research or investigating institutions. Till that time, this ISO certificate was not awarded to any other department of Govt. of India. Apart from it, there were many discussions on this topic in different papers, magazines and televisions. Srijukta N. Vittal, the Commissioner (CVC) had pointed out that this process should be implemented in other organizations. He had attended the following international conferences when he was posted as the Chief Vigilance Officer (CVO) in Indian Oil Corporation.

In the year 1999, he represented India in an international conference held at the Atlanta in United States of America. It was a workshop on social and developmental work in America. The topic of his discourse was good management and good direction in Govt. companies.

He was invited by Fordham University, New-York in the year 2002. He had presented a meaningful article on "corruptions impact on the organised system" in that international Summit.

During the period from 2003 to 2005 Dr. Satpathy was posted at Delhi as Chief Vigilance Officer (CVO) of Oil and Natural Gas Corporation (ONGC). He continued in that post till May 2005. There were material improvements in the working procedure or the department due to a lot of changes made in it. The then Chief Vigilance Commissioner Shri P. Shankar had appreciated all these activities.

In 2005 CE, when he was Chief Vigilance Officer of ONGC, the editor and chief executive officer of international "Forbes" magazine had invited him. This Conference was held in London in the month of June, 2004. Dr. Satpathy had delivered his speech on "Ease of doing business in India."

At this time he was selected as the vice-president of Indian Weightlifting Federation. This federation is affiliated with International Weightlifting Federation, Asian Weightlifting Federation and Commonwealth Weightlifting Federation.

In the year 2005 -2006, Shri Satpathy had got promotion as Additional Director General of Central Industrial Security Force. Industrial Security Force is a para military organization. This organisation works under the Home ministry of Govt. of India. He had served in this post up to May 2006. There were 95,000 persons working in this Industrial Security Force. They were deployed for the security of almost all the civil airports in India. Apart from it, the safety, responsibility of national memorial monuments (i.e. Tajmahal, Lalkilla etc.) were entrusted to them. Besides this, they had taken the security charge of important Leaders. The policies and combative tactics of Central Industrial Security Force (CISF) were determined while he was the Additional Director.

2005 CE – when Shriman Satpathy was the additional Director General of Central Industrial Security Force (CISF), he had delivered his Lecture in a regional meeting on "Instant Performance Boost". This programme was organised by National Academy of Industrial Safety, Hyderabad and Nepal Institute of Earth Science. The delegation from seven countries (i.e. Philippines, Bangladesh, Nepal etc.) participated in it. The CISF is the first systematic organisation in handling national emergency.

After completion of his deputation period, he came back to Uttar Pradesh and posted as Director General in Dr B.R. Ambedkar Police Academy, Moradabad following his promotion in 2006 CE. This academy, one of the oldest institutions in India, was established in 1902 CE. When he was the director of this institution, all the police personnel starting from I.P.S. to Sub Inspectors were coming for training. A police museum, one golf field, ladies officer hostel, an auditorium and different police buildings were constructed during his tenure as director. These are not small things to be accomplished. He had transformed the U.P. Police to a proud institution. Many student organisations, tourists as well as eminent persons used to visit this Institution.

Government of India had entrusted him to investigate all the details relating to Godhra incident of Gujurat when he was in the Special Investigation Team (SIT) during April 2008 to April 2009. The investigation procedures of this Godhra incident were conducted at the SIT office situated in Gandhinagar (Ahmedabad).

Shri Satpathy was appointed as an advisor in Petronet L.N.G. (Liquid Natural Gas) at New Delhi. Petronet L.N.G. Ltd. is one of the best institutions of India and it imports around 76% gas of country's requirement.

OTHER UNIQUE HONOURS

On 11th July 2008, the North Odisha University (NOU) situated at Baripada, Mayurbhanj had felicitated Dr. Satpathy with "The glorious boy of Mayurbhanj" award. This award was presented to him on his excellence in the field of Literature, music composing, art and spiritualism. Here I want to inform that Baripada is the paternal place of Dr. Satpathy.

On 23rd January 2009, the old students Association of Ravenshaw Collegiate School, Cuttack had decorated him with the "Student's Pride" honour. This honour is given to any person for his contribution in the sphere of Society,

Literature, music and education in national and international level.

On 17th April 2011, at Bhubaneswar, the "Mepal and Dr. D.N. Rath foundation" had bestowed him with "Mahapurush Jagannath Dash" award for his devotional and religious writings. Fortunately, I was present in that function.

In 2011 CE, the Sai Inspiration Trust, Mumbai congratulated Shri Satpathy for propagating and spreading the fame of Sai Baba remarkably. This programme was onganised magnificently by both Star T.V. and Sai Inspiration Trust. On this occasion, Star TV and a music organisation "Mallik ek Sura Anek" had arranged a music festival on 12th May.

On 2nd July 2011, Shriman Satpathy was hunoured by the American Odia Society of Plano, Texas, on their 42nd annual function, for his priceless contribution to the humanity, spiritual values, divine quality and Literacy Skills.

The "Tapasya Sangeet Academy" of Deogarh in Jharkhand had conferred him with the "Baba Baidyanath Sangeeta Ratna" title in 2011 CE. This award is given only for exemplary contribution in music.

On 10th November 2011, the "Odia Pua" Society of New Delhi had adorned him with "Odisha Ratna" title. This title is generally given to famous people and his famous works were his contribution to the classical music, excellence in Literature Social services and spiritual insight.

On 25th February 2012, on the occasion of 15th Convocation ceremony of Tirupati University the prestigious D.Litt. Degree was conferred upon Dr. Satpathy by the national Sanskrit University. This university is a famous Learning Centre of Sanskrit Language in India. This prestigious D.Litt. Degree is given to very few people. This degree is given to Shriman Satpathy for his divine quality, spiritual expertise, special contribution in protecting the sovereignty of the country, dissemination of education and participation in national and international conferences etc.

On 26th February 2012, Delhi Astro study circle had rewarded him for "achievement of Life's objective". The spheres he had worked were (1) Astrology (2) Astronomy (3) music and (4) Sai Consciousness.

On 8th April 2012, he was presented with "Prarthana Samman" by the Prarthana T.V. This TV channel is a devotional music channel and had imparted their first "Prarthana Samman" award to Shriman Satpathy.

In May 2012, the Berhampur University had felicitated him with L.L.D. degree for his valuable contribution in the field of classical and devotional music, expertise in astrology and astronomy, advances in the development of Sai consciousness, propagation of Sai philosophy in different countries etc. This degree is generally given to eminent scholars, charitable persons and persons with extra-ordinary contribution in one or more fields. In 2014 CE, Dr. Satpathy was honoured with D.Sc. degree by Sikhya O Anusandhan (SOA) University, Bhubaneswar for his contribution to the society, expansion of Sai leela in different countries, construction of Sai temples in foreign countries and explaining clearly to different class of people about Sai concept. The excellent achievements of Dr. Satpathy in other fields are also reflected in this award. Dr. Satpathy is the first Sai devotee who has established many Sai temples in India and also in foreign countries (i.e. England, America, Australia, Canada and some countries in Africa). He had set up his first Sai temple in Chennai. The Sai temples of Bhubaneswar, Berhampur, Baragarh and Sambalpur are controlled by Chennai trust. Dr. Satpathy is the chief architecture of expansion of Sai consciousness and Construction for hundreds Sai temples. His endeavours to establish these temples are unparalleled. He is not only establishing the temples but also advising the management of the institutions regarding the maintenance of the temples and method of worshiping to Baba. Further he discusses with the trustees about smooth functioning of other special activities. Some time back, there was a meeting in Bhubaneswar where representatives of many trusts were participated. All the Sai devotees of India and abroad are used to take part in different activities of the temples. The people of all religions like Hindu, Muslim, Sikh, Christian etc go to Sai temples for worshiping and participate in Bhajan programme This indicates that we all are one and our owner is also one.

DELIVERING SOCIAL JUSTICE

Dr. Satpathy is a diligent person who is trying to provide social justice to every class of people. Of course it is not possible in all cases but his attitude remains unchanged. To lead a life in a difficult circumstance and accordingly face the situation is the desire of a true man. As per Guruji, the gift to the society by Smt. Shruti Mohapatra (i.e. trying to establish the mentally ill boys and girls in the society) of Bhubaneswar, is the real adoration of Sai Baba. It may be our credit to construct many temples and worship regularly but service to mankind is the best and noble action. It does not mean to collect donations from the devotees in the name of service to mankind. As per the opinion of Dr. Satpathy, the temples are the place of worship where we all take refuge before the God and praise Him by singing devotional songs. The first and foremost work of the Debalaya (Temple) is to propagate His greatness. To use the donations received from the devotees for own benefit is the most disgusting work. It is not only the viewpoint of the Guruji but it is a mischievous act. No doubt about it. Further, it has been observed that the people are comparing between the temples. Like, that temple is very beautiful, this temple is nothing before that. I have been hearing so many real and unreal comparisons like this since I came in contact with Sai temples. Even the interest and energy of the devotees to take the priest and other employees from one temple to other is not noticed in any other organization. This is my observance only. There is a scarcity of understanding among each other in today's world. We usually argue to prove our point but this argument has no stability due to emotional disturbances. Most of the times the situation created by a mistake or misunderstanding can be eradicated by your own will power.

The purpose of writing these things is that Guruji Satpathy has explained in detail in different books and magazines regarding commitment of the Sadgurus, the understanding between different communities, helping the poor and handicapped persons etc. We declare ourselves as Sai devotees but forget the advice of Sai Baba. Dada J.P. Vaswani has told that we blame others without understanding many things. We not only blame them but also criticize them. As per his saying, one lady used to purchase vegetables from a vegetable vendor every day. One day the vegetable vendor did not come. The Lady had abused and offended him when he came back after some days. When asked, the vegetable vendor had expressed that he is sorry for it but what could I do? Yesterday my mother expired and I had to go for her funeral rites. After hearing this, that lady felt ashamed. One should not reach on conclusion suddenly without hearing or understanding properly. Many times we presume all beggars as fakes without knowing the differences between real beggars and fake ones. May be some of them actually lead a very difficult life and do not get any help from anybody. It is hard to imagine, the number of houses destroyed in villages by the cyclone Phailin. We, on behalf of Berhampur Sai temple, had gone to some villages to distribute cooked food and drinking water. All were looking 5E@5ctantly. There was no difficulty in distributing the food and water due to the help of police personnel. When we had gone for distributing the blankets, we were not able to know to whom we would give, because all the villagers were of lower income group and the houses were no longer habitable due to flood water entering the houses. When we gave a blanket to an old woman, she returned it and said "what shall I do with the blanket when my house was consumed by the cyclone? Can anybody tell this a house where there is no place for cooking; the roof has blown away and the floor is extremely damp?" While crying the old woman had narrated these things. Immediately, we informed the other organisations to help her. Actually, the conditions of the villages near seashore were almost same. It is beyond one's imagination to feel the pains inflicted by the furry of the storm. One generous person has built a thatched house for the old woman. Guruji Shri Chandra Bhanu Satpathy always gives importance to humanity and humanism. He knows the path leading to divinity and guides people accordingly.

The most excellent work done during the tenure of Shri Satpathy is to help the real beggars, leprosy patients and disabled persons. Once he escorted some leprosy patients, sitting in front of Sai temple at Tankapani Road, by holding their hands He helped them to take their meals inside the temple. He himself also served them. This activity of him indicates that one should love the Leprosy patients instead of detesting them. Sai Baba is satisfied by this. The devotees may be astonished. Shri Satpathy has advised to read "Shri Sai Satcharitra" always consistently. His own writings on the reading of "Shri Sai Satcharitra" are appended below.

A BRIEF NOTE BY GURUJI ON "SHRI SAI SATCHARITRA"

I had read in detail different Purans, Upanishads, Bhagabat, Gorakh Samhita, Gheranda Samhita and biography of many saints. I had also perused Bible, Koran and many texts written on Buddhism and Sikhism. I had kept many photo copies of them with me too. I had established a feeling of instant intimacy with these holy books.

These feelings or emotions were initiated when I was residing in a Govt. Bunglow at Netaji Nagar, New Delhi during the year 1989-90. I had no satisfaction even after studying deeply and in detail. It was as if I was searching something else from the most inner corner of my soul. Perhaps, in my subconscious mind, I was seeking for the answers of questions like "how my previous births did I have and why I took the rebirth?" I had studied many civilisations; I also read the books written on Pyramids of Egypt and its dead persons, the books authored by the Tibetan Lamas on dead men and many books in Hindi, English, Sanskrit and my mother tongue odia written on this subject. I had read mot only once or twice but also many times still, I did not get peace. I was not able to know, what exactly I was searching. I had also practiced Kriya y>g0, Dhyana yog0, Bhakti yog0, Hat0 yog0, Black magic and different methods of worships. I could not get full hearted satisfaction though I used to get temporary contentment out of these. It seemed to me that I was floating in the stream of the unconscious.

While investigating aimlessly like this, suddenly I realised that I should come out of this mind-ruled knowledgeable forest area and reach my destination. I felt that the Nature, rivers, stars and my near and dear ones are waving their hands and calling me with affection and admiration. I entered into a different world by tearing apart the shackles of my mind, where a simple, fluid, easy lifestyle existed.

This was possible only when Shri Sainath Maharaj blessed me. I did not even hear his name till 1989. I felt as if Shri Sainath appeared in my life to repay the loans of all my previous births or as though the result of all the virtuous deeds done by me in the previous births became manifest. It appears that the God to whom my father, grandfather and forefathers had worshiped for thousand years has blessed one of their descendants and favoured him with their gracious Blessings on the fruits of piety of their long devotion.

I had nothing to say more, when the Guru Maharaj was enthroned in my heart. With great Surprise, I continued to observe as a silent spectator, the sudden changes occurred in my thoughts and consciousness. After receiving the Blessings of Shri Sai Nath, I totally got immersed in learning the arati of Baba and a strong desire enveloped me to hear this at all times. The synchronization of words by Dasganu Maharaj was very simple and fascinating.

"Raham Najar karo ab more Sai,
Tumbin Nahin Mujhe, ma bap Bhai,
Me Andha hun Banda Tumhara,
me na janu Alla Illahee".

"Oh! Sai Maharaj, have mercy on me. Because you are my mother, father, brother everything. I am following you like a blind man. You are everything to me. I cannot think any other God except you." I used to perform arati two or three times in a day in front of Baba's image. I bought and read all the books available in Shiridi and Delhi; it was due to my much interest to know more and more regarding Baba. At that time, not so many books were published on Baba like today; only ten to twelve books in Hindi and English were available. In 1989, while returning from Shiridi, I brought the Hindi translation of "Shri Sai Sat Charitra" with me. Somebody had told me that Hemadpant, a devotee with little education, has written this book; there was direct grace and Blessings of Shri Sai. I had some idea on the life of Baba when I read the book for the first time. The super-natural incidents in his life were described magnificently in detail in this book. The more I read the book, more divine bliss I felt inside me. This type of experience was never experienced by me before. At times, I used to read the same episode for 8 to 10 times to fully understand and feel the heavenly activities (Leela Khela) of Baba. Are the descriptions written in the book true? This question had perturbed me again and again.

Is it true that the cholera cannot touch the periphery of the village by scattering a sack of hand-grinded wheat on the circumference of the village? Is it possible to ignite a lamp by water? Can a person control the fire or stop the rain as per his wish? I felt it baseless and fictional stories like the incidents described in Hindu mythology. I thought perhaps one of his adherent disciples narrated the supernatural stories exaggeratedly to propagate the greatness of his Guru. But some of the incidents seemed to be true to me. Then my body was trembling and I was shivering with weird excitement. I was thinking from the bottom of my heart, O' my adorable Sai, if these are true then why I did not take birth before some years to see your divine deeds (Leelakhela)? At times the flow of Love was so intense that I used to prostrate for a long period before the photo of Sainath after closing the doors and windows. I could not speak anything. Only echoes were heard from the remote corner of the heart "I prostrate before thee Sainath.... Shri Sainath". On that moment I wished to breathe my last by uttering this name repeatedly. But next moment the intelligence played its own game. The fickle mind dragged me in to the reality of the troubled world. Anyhow, I had controlled my mind and continued to read the Sai Satcharitra. After I completed 42nd chapter, my chest palpitated wildly. Up till now, you were hearing the life story of Baba. Now, please hear intently regarding Baba's leaving of his mortal body.

"Leaving the body by Baba" – As soon as he read this phrase, his heart had broken in deep pain. Till this chapter, he was reading His birth history so intently that his entire consciousness has been enveloped with an impression that, as if, Baba is alive. I assumed myself as a part of his life in the innermost corner of his heart and Sai became my father and dearest friend. In the environment like this, the time stands still because while reading Sai Satchritra, the consciousness of time had disappeared in him.

What he has expressed on "Leaving the body by

Baba" – on the moment I came to know – Baba left his mortal body, I trembled, my eyes were moist and there was a choking sensation in me. Tears were rolling down my eyes continuously. Automatically, I knelt down and kissed the holy feet of Baba and begged before him by holding his photo tightly to my chest. Baba, Please do not do like this. I prostrated before him and courageously continued reading in that disturbed mental state. I read "on 28th September 1918, Baba was suffering from slight fever. That fever continued for 2/3 days. But after that Baba left eating any food. As a result, he became very weak gradually. After 17 days i.e. on 15th October 1918, at 2:30 pm Baba left his physical body. (Shri Sai Satcharitra - 42 chapters)

While I was reading this, my heart felt as if it would be torn apart into thousand pieces due to extreme sadness. I was feeling helpless and powerless. I felt as though, I have lost my father and became fatherless. Again it was written, before two years of this incident (i.e. in 1916), Baba had informed regarding leaving of his body. Before his Mahaprayan, Baba had donated nine rupees, his last resource, to Laxmibai, one of his devotees. He had directed all his disciples to take their food as he knew very well that they will not eat anything after his demise. This kindness towards his devotees was deeply moved me emotionally. I was bidding him farewell mentally, in this moment of extreme sadness.

I prostate before thee Sainath, I prostrate before thee. I told him from my heart – "O' Sainath, O' Incarnation of kindness, I am dumb struck by observing your kindness. My life will be blessed and my soul will get peace if I will get an opportunity even in thousand lives to be a dust particle under your feet.

It is mentioned in Shri Sai Satcharitra – The news of Baba's Mahaprayan had spread around Shiridi village like a forest fire. Men, women, old men, children all were running towards Masjid and began to mourn in different ways. Some were crying loudly, some rolled on the dusty road. Some were even senseless. Who will console them? Who will describe their unbearable sorrow ? (Shri Sai Satcharita – 42nd chapter)

While reading this heart touching description, the tears from my eyes rolled down continuously. Perhaps the people of Shiridi were weeping just like this. I felt as if I died that moment and stood up again in front of Baba's mortal body. I could observe Baba's body resting on Bayaji's shoulder. I was beholding with tearful eyes that my ideals have been passed away with my God and my Lord. I continued my reading with deep pain and depression. His "departure from the mortal body" is subject to a universal law. He is present in all living and non-living beings and he is the consciousness of all the creatures. Those who have surrendered completely before His holy feet and worship regularly, still experience divine happiness now and it will continue like so. (Shri Sai Satcharitra – 43-44 chapters)

After going through it, my disturbed mind calmed down to some extent. Depression was also reduced substantially. Yet, at times the memory of Baba's Last moment pierced my heart like a sharp iron rod and then I become depressed deeply. Even when I remember those incidents now, I am engulfed by sorrow and absolute helplessness. Shri Sai Satcharitra had made me very close to Baba. As a result, I had received his divine Blessings. I became bound by an unbreakable bond with him.

The life history of Sai Baba, the stories he has told on

animals and birds and his sayings are extremely wonderful. These are providing peace and satisfaction as well as both knowledge and science on worldly and spiritual levels to the human being suffering from pain and sorrow in this world. The teachings of Sai Baba, like the verses of vedas, are so beautiful and educative that all the wishes of a devotee are fulfilled if he is focused on listening and singing it. He can get peace from meditation and divine blessings from performing Astanga yoga and also get the eternal salvation (Shri Sai Satcharitra – 2nd chapter)

Guruji continued to read Shri Sai Satcharitra regularly for 3 to 4 years. He had completed the reading (Parayan) of Shri Sai Satcharitra in the night of Mahashibaratri in 1993 by lighting a lamp in front of the photo of Sai Baba when he had gone to Shiridi. He purchased many Shri Sai Satcharitra books in Hindi and English and distributed them among the people.

We get some special information about life through Shri Sai Satcharitra by examining its greatness from philosophical or spiritual angles which provide assistance to devotees irrespective of religious denominations. The devotees like Mhalsapathi, Hemadpant, Tatyakote Patil, Laxmibai Shinde, Das Ganu, Kaka Saheb Dixit, Bapu Saheb Jog, Shama etc. who had got the opportunity to spend most of their life time with Baba had many experiences like this. Some intellectuals like Dada Saheb Khaparde have recorded their memories in their diaries during their stay in Shiridi. The incidents described there are a vivid account of their rare experience of attaining Baba's closeness. The characters and incidents transcribed in this book are not out imaginary at all. Those are real. Baba had recorded these facts through Davolkar by providing him with intrinsic motivation. Baba once told him "I am writing my biography." As a result of faith and confidence in the heart of my devotees, the practice of listening to my teachings and divine activities (Leelas) will bring joy and inner vision. (Shri Sai Satcharitra – 2nd chapter)

THE SPECIALTY OF SHRI SAI SATCHARITRA

1. This book was the first and foremost book on Shri Sai Baba which was published in verse form in Marathi. This was written during the life time of Baba with his blessings.
2. This was translated into simple Hindi, so that common men can understand it.
3. There are much more truths in this book than the knowledge gained by reading Vedas and Geeta, because here all the characters and incidents are based on facts and is written down systematically by many disciples.
4. Due to use of simple Hindi, all will understand it easily. There are very few people seen nowadays, who can realise the essence of books written in Sanskrit.
5. All the substances of scriptures like Vedas, Geeta, Yogabasista are available in Shri Sainath's biography.
6. There is no need of more books or materials to understand the God and spiritualism which are explained in very simple manner in Shri Sai Satcharitra. It is described in such easy and convenient way that the readers will feel that these are related to events of their past births.

Therefore, the main duty of all Sai devotees is to read Shri Sai Satcharitra and fully absorb the gist of it. The more one reads this book, the closer one gets to Baba and all his fears and doubts will disappear. It is also observed that if a devotee is in crisis and eagerly opens any page of Shri Sai Satcharitra and prays Baba with full faith and devotion, then he will get the solution to his crisis in that page only. Many devotees have achieved their desired results by reading (Parayan) the Shri Sai Satcharitra only for a week.

For the information of all the Sai devotees, we append below the correct method of reading Shri Sai Satcharitra.

1) Please arrange a Shri Sat Satcharitra book in any language it you want to read it. Keep it, after wrapping it by a piece of new cloth, in front of Baba's photo or statue as a holy object.

2) Whether at home or out, please read some pages of it before going to bed. Every disciple should bring Baba to the realm of his imagination just before sleeping.

3) At the time of crisis, the Shri Sai Satcharitra should be read as mentioned in the book. If possible, the reading (Parayan) should be started from Thursday or any other sacred days i.e. Rama Nabami, Dussehra, Guru Purnima, Janmastami, Mahashibaratri etc. on the 7th day, when the parayan is completed, the poors should be served at the house or temple.

4) This should be read in an isolated corner of the temple or in front of photo, oil painting or idol of Baba. If some others are present, then it can be read before them or with them jointly. To read it always as a group activity should be encouraged.

5) This should be read at any time in a Sai temple until sunset on any holy day. As the God's name is chanted, the devotees will chant it sweetly in unison

continuously. Competitions may be arranged in the temples among the Children based on the questions answers on Shri Sai Satcharitra.

6) Devotees who are old, sick and close to death should get more opportunity of listening recital of Shri Sai Charitra. The more the opportunity the greater is the peaceful condition for them.

7) Shri Sai Satcharitra is available in Shiridi at affordable price. So, all the devotees visiting Shiri should purchase some books and distribute them to others free of charge.

8) If one relies on the recitation of Shri Sai Satcharitra with faith in times of distress, he not only finds a way of healing but also finds solace and satisfaction in it.

My prayer to Shri Sainath is to kindly bless all the devotees who are reading this scripture. May Sai Nath help them to see the spiritual light within as He has inspired Hemadpant to write this book. All the Sai devotees should treat this Sai Satcharitra as Geeta and Bible.

According to Guruji, everything that happens on this world is Maya's game. If what we think is done, then we think that all our wishes have been fulfilled. In the cinema hall many pictures seems alive. On seeing them we also laugh with their Laughter, Cry with their crying and get overwhelmed with their sadness. But actually the cinema screen is the only truth; others are the trap of illusion (Maya). We cannot see anything if the screen is removed. Many people do not understand the game of truth and untruth. Be it jewelry or pottery, these are just aberrations. In the same way the differences in the disorder that competes for one causes the other to suffer. This concept is above our consciousness because we all remain subservient to maya. By getting rid of it, we can view the heavenly figure of the Param Brahma. Sai Baba is a medium whose help and blessings can propel the devotees to a higher level in spiritual world.

We always think about our well-being and happiness. Each part of this feeling is related to self interest. Can we even think to give the food, served to us, to a hungry dog? Perhaps much courage and effort are required to do this work. First to get the permission of the person who cooked, thinking about for how many people the food is cooked and putting them in to practice are complimentary to each other. Apart from it, is it our duty to feed the stray dogs? Many questions arise in our mind like this. Serving the patients, leading the blinds, guiding those who have lost their way, donating blood etc are public works. We all know this but do not do it. The reasons for not doing it come to our mind automatically. There is a Government and Govt. enterprises to do it. Why should we get involved in this?

Now Shri Sai Satcharitra in odia are available in all Sai temples in Odisha. Guruji Shri Satpathy has written it for personal reading as well as collective reading of this book by the devotees.

VARIOUS WORKS OF GURUJI SHRI CHANDRA BHANU SATPATHY

Shri Chandra Bhanu Satpathy is addressed as Guruji by many people and is stated as the true devotee of Sai Baba. Of course, he does not want to call himself a glorious, divine powered and visionary person before any one. At times he also prohibits the use of such addressing. He advises us to write his name always as Chandra Bhanu Satpathy without any prefix or suffix. This is his own. Even if he is called as Shri Chandra Bhanu, the calling seems awkward. So, in my opinion, he should be addressed as Guruji Shri Satpathy.

Meanwhile many universities have felicitated him with L.L.D. and D.Ltt. degrees. Therefore, some changes in the addressing process are desirable. Whatever it may be, Guruji Shri Satpathy has nothing to say about it. He always tells that the cosmic master, be it God or Sai Baba wants the best for all. We all are able-bodied not imperfect and should not think of ourselves as incomplete, ineligible or disabled. This category of people should lead a happy life with their real identity.

What does a disabled person want? What will the society give him? What is the expectation of these people from the society? etc. etc. From my experience these disabled persons do not want anything. Because, they do not know the difference between good and bad. It is our duty to provide better reservation system, so that special environment can be established. We should provide special privileges and giving special rights to them. But it is reported that such people who are identified as persons with disabilities get very few opportunities. I know from my own experience that the special services, special rights and a chance to live a better life are offered in some old age homes - These are all smoke screens. Nothing happens like this. When asked they reply that no grant has come from the government so far. This is the internal affairs of the old age home. The other one is an ashram or institution for the handicapped. Generally, the govt. aid does not come much to these institutions. If these institutions built for the differently abled are controlled by some well known voluntary people or groups who have devoted themselves to social service, then these institutions will improve significantly. I know some people have created such an institution and earned a lot of money from the centre and abroad. Are these funds actually being used for the disabled persons? Disabled means, he cannot tell anything. How can he tell whether the money received has actually been spent on them or not? Of course, this type of unethical work is not done everywhere. The activities of the institutions built on public or private funds are questionable. But the future of the institutions created voluntarily, without the help of Govt. are bright. We all should help these organisations in different ways. I can tell from my experience that there are many institutions in Bhubaneswar which provide all kinds of moral and psychological support to the inmates to improve their future. Rather than enriching them only with wealth, sensitivity emanating from the heart is appreciated.

Guruji Shri Satpathy is attached with many institutions like this. He does not believe in mercy and favour. Actually, these two works are the enemy of any helpless man. It is estimated that 10% people of our country are disabled, helpless, orphan, chronic patients and unable to live. Three things (i.e. food, cloth and house) are essentially necessary for their survival. Apart from it "the desire to live" is on the top of all. Many aged persons are trying their level best to survive even if they are on the door step of their death. God helps these people to maintain their life without depending on others. It is our duty to ensure that all disabled persons do not feel that they are living on the mercies of others.

THE PHILANTHROPIC PROGRAMMES OF GURUJI

Guruji Shriman Satpathy has always tried to uplift the less privileged sections of the society to the upper echelons of the society. He also takes the help of others for this noble cause. Hundred of private charitable organisations have been formed due to his inspiration and guidance. All these organisations can also manage the philanthropic programmes efficiently.

The philanthropic activities include –

Shriman Satpathy is a patron of "Swabhiman", an organisation in Bhubaneswar. The purpose of this organisation is to serve the disabled persons and take responsibility for their survival as human beings in future. The main aim of this institution is to bring the handicapped people of the society (i.e. persons who who lost their Limbs, physically deformed people, blind, deaf, dumb and people with mental disorder), to the main stream of the society - For this, tremendous efforts are required and only trying is not sufficient but to study their desires in a cool mind is highly necessary. The most important thing is that children of all these classes should be brought up in such a way that they do not feel helpless. Shriman Satpathy is also a patron of another organisation "Anjali" (which is another organised body like "Swabhiman"). On 27th February 2010, there was a cultural programme "we can dance" organised by the inmates of "Swabhiman" institution in Sai International School. The programmes of dancing and singing by many disabled children and youths were conducted smoothly. Dr. Shruti Mohapatra, the Managing Director of "Swabhiman", had supervised the programme herself. In fact, the programme was so fascinating that we were dazzled by the performance. It is astonishing to think that the programme "We can dance" was actually performed by the physically and mentally handicapped boys and girls. Many spectators (i.e. writers, film stars, social workers, students, teachers and the guardians, parents of the students of the organisation) had attended this special programme. Even the video operators and media personnel had participated in it. This programme was also telecast in TV channels. During these programmes, Guruji Satpathy had announced a donation of one lakh rupees to "Swabhiman" organisation. This one lakh rupees was given to him as an honorarium by "The Meple and D. N. Rath Foundation" for his expertise in Odia religious Literature. He was also honoured by Mohapurush Jagannath Das Samman at Bhubaneswar. On 18th March 2012, "Swaviman" and "Anjali" were organised a function together. The function was to show the competence of the handicapped boys and girls in music, dance and art. Shri Chandra Bhanu Satpathy, the patron of Sai International School which is a very advanced institution in all respect, announced that one person would be employed full time and two others on a temporally basis. The meaning of this announcement was to create an environment for them and employ such people to Lead a normal life without depending on others. Again he declared that in the future many such favourable circumstances would be created so that this class of people would be able to stand on their own feet.

HELPING THE UNDER-PRIVILEGED PEOPLE

"Sukanya" is a registered private organisation formed to help the under privileged. Generally this organisation had been working for the benefit of children, the aged and women of this under-proviledged class. Guruji Shri Chandra Bhanu Satpathy is the chief patron and advisor of this "Sukanya". The main purpose of this is to do some developmental work for the people staying in the slums in Haryana. It was decided to start this organisation in 1998. But this organisation became operational in February 2001. The work was started by the members, volunteers and some well-wishers of this institution. The view of "Sukanya" like doing benevolent works or spreading religious sentiments motivated others to do good deeds. Religious consciousness and unwavering desire to do some good work may bind all people together. There was a dream visualized together by a team of doctors, entrepreneurs, news and communication staff, Govt. and private people, social workers etc. Its main objective is to promote good health and better society. The main activity of this organisation is to solve various problems of local people by collaborating with the Govt. and getting different aids for them. It is capable of bringing together thousands of people, especially women and adolescent boys, to the main-stream of the society. Of course, it took 13 years to reach that level. About five lakh people have been benefited by opening "Sukanya" health centres and conducting health camps on various diseases like diabetes, heart disease, gynecology etc. One of the main tasks of this organisation is to open health centres in villages far from the towns and educate the people about health care. On 5th November 2004, the mobile clinic made it possible to provide treatment at the convenience of the general public. In 2005 "Sukanya" opened a branch of physiotherapy and could ease the pain of patients with bone diseases. Other humanitarian aid of "Sukanya" includes Tsunami, Odisha Super Cyclone, Gujurat earth quake etc. In all these operations, it took a major part in rescue and rehabilitation of about 1000 families. Many school buildings were repaired and were made suitable places for teaching. Apart from it, the re-training of the trainees is a unique idea. This thought was put into action by Shri Chandra Bhanu Satpthy. As a result, every plan was completed smoothly.

ALL KINDS OF HELP TO THE LEPERS

The "Jeevan Deep Kusthashram Colony" is situated in R.K. Puram, New Delhi. Under the auspices of Shri Chandra Bhanu Satpathy, the temple and its community hall were repaired and a Shiridi Sai temple was built inside the temple. This temple was inaugurated by Guruji on 15th June 1995. The devotees have been giving food and clothing to the leper patients in the courtyard of the temple. Other social activities were also held in temple courtyard. At the behest of Guruji Satpathy or under his patronage, food, clothing, medicines and medical aid are being given to the Lepers in timely manner. For almost 20 years, Guruji has been visiting the Leprosy homes (Kusthashrams) in Modinagar, Gaziabad and understanding the pros and cons of Leprosy patients. Not just this Leprosy home (Kusthashram), Guruji himself visited almost all the Leprosy homes in Delhi and enquired the needs of the patients. Thousands of Leprosy patients did not face any difficulties in getting free medicines, food and clothes due to the sincere efforts by Guruji.

Guruji Shri Chandra Bhanu Satpathy had instituted many charitable institutions in India and outside India (America, Australia, England, Canada and South Africa). The activities of these organizations are to distribute medicines, provide free medical treatment, organise medical camps, feed the needy and distribute clothes etc. The aim of these charitable institutions is to improve the social conditions in all states of India.

REGULATIONS OF CHARITABLE INSTITUTIONS

These institutes conduct free medical camps to diagnose various diseases and arrange for the treatment of these diseases to control them. To distribute free medicines to the poor people is included in this work. Till now 10,000 people are benefited under this Scheme.

Apart from this, Moradabad's (U.P.) charitable institution has also opened a veterinary clinic. This clinic provides free treatment and medicines. This programme has been going on till now under the supervision of Shri Satpathy. By establishing this hospital animals are being treated.

On the instruction of Guruji Shri Chandra Bhanu Satpathy, a number of health institutions both allopathic and homeopathic Centres were opened. No negligence was seen in these two hospitals till now. Apart from health services, these institutions have been donating food and clothing to the poor. Their services are inspiring in the field of education for about twenty years. Free treatments of thousands of patients are being done by about 100 hospitals. These works are continuing till now by the instructions of Shri Satpathy.

These institutions had distributed food, clothes, medicines and other necessary things to the affected people of Odisha during the super cyclone, Tsumami and other natural calamities in 1999 by the direction of Shri Satpathy. This was not a small thing. Even during this great cyclone (12.10.2013), Berhampore Sai temple organisation distributed various types of cooked food, blankets and dry food in these areas (Gopalpur, Chamakhandi and port area) with its limited resources.

ASTRONOMY

Between 1989 to 1992, Shriman Satpathy was the first to initiate applied research on Pyramidology in India. Its main purpose was to diagnose and treat patients with the help of pyramids. Many doctors also helped him in this experiment. The underlying purpose was to cure the incurable diseases. At that time, the issue was fully covered in the national TV channels and the national news papers. Shriman Satpathy was also well versed in astrology. He was able to foretell people all the events related to astrology for about 20 years. Researching on a subject matter was his hobby, not his business. He was awarded "Life time achievement" award for his research work and contribution to astrology.

HIS CONTRIBUTION TO THE SPREAD OF EDUCATION

A – A Shirdi Sai Baba Public School was first established in Moradabad, Uttar Pradesh and he is the main patron of it. Value based education is better than bookish education. This idea must raise the standard of education. No doubt about it. This is also the opinion of Shriman Satpathy. As per this opinion, he made arrangements for free education of talented poor children in some Schools.

He is still the main patron of Bhubaneswar Sai International School. Due to his directions, enthusiasm and motivation, the school was able to stand up in a short time. The school has now proved, not only in Odisha but also in entire India, better than many higher level Schools in terms of higher education and various departments.

Under the instruction of Shriman Satpathy, a children's Sai Group was born. The "Sai ka Angan" was created by this group in 2007. This "Sai ka Angan" is a religious place and the principal purpose of it is to worship and to improve the art and culture. The Supervision of these were the responsibility of "Sai Prakash spiritual and charitable trust" of which Satpathy is the patron. The main objective of this forum was to inculcate human values and clarity in the minds of young children so that they can become good citizens of the society and country in future. The purpose of this forum is to uplift the humanity. Baba was also encouraging all to do this work. Many children (more than 200) are participating in the programme of this forum due to the functioning of this group. This group under the supervision of Shri Chandra Bhanu Satpathy has become a model for all. Gradually, the other trusts are coming forward to participate with it.

B) In April 2004, Shri Chandra Bhanu Satpathy had delivered a summarising speech in Shri Venkateswar University, Tirupati about his "Mulya Jadita Shikhya" which is "value based education" in English. Very few people get a chance to deliver a speech like this. This speech was organised in memory of the former Chief Minister of Andhra Pradesh. Scholars like Professor Nurul Hassan also spoke in this university.

Shri Chandra Bhanu Satpathy had delivered a Summative speech in the gathering of Sanskrit scholars and students. The speech was about "the need for religious sentiment in today's society". This meeting was organised at Rastriya Sanskrut Bidyapith, Tirupati on 26th August 2007. Tirupati spiritual centre and National Sanskrit University were among the organisers.

At the end a summary Lecture was given to the students on the topic related to profession by Shriman Satpathy. He also gave some advice to school and college students about getting and doing jobs.

CONTRIBUTION TO LITERATURE BY GURUJI SATPATHY

On 17th April 2011, he was honoured with "Mahapurus Jagannath Dash Samman" at Bhubaneswar. Guruji later donated the proceeds (one Lakh rupees) of this award to the "Swaviman" organisation. This award is given to the authors of Odia religious literature.

On 25th February 2012, the National Sanskrit School Authority conferred the D.Lit. (Honorary) degree to Shriman Chandra Bhanu Satpathy on the convocation ceremony of the university. The university awards this degree only to those who have made a great contribution to the education sector of the country or to any person who has achieved an extraordinary success. This degree is usually given at a convocation to a person distinguished for achievement in the Sanskrit Language or special religious work. The university authorities determine the person who will be eligible for this honour. The degree has been given to Shriman Satpathy for his teaching of religious philosophy, nationalism, for the spread of education, for facilitating the teachings of Sai Philosophy in national and international organisations and for setting up various educational institutions etc.

On 2nd May 2012, on the occasion of their 17th convocation, the Berhampur University had awarded him a prestigious L.L.D. degree for his outstanding contribution to the society.

During the period 1964 to 1968, while reading in the college, Guruji Shri Satpathy was writing many short stories. They were humorous and satirical writings which were published in Dagar, Asantakali, Jhankar and Revenshaw College magazines.

1968-1988 – During this period all his satirical writings were published in various magazines in Odia and Hindi.

In 1980, an Odia satirical book "Hasyankur" was published by Dagar Press, Cuttack.

1982 – None of us could believe that he could create such beautiful Comic and Satirical Literatures. But till now we have not got the opportunity to read the complete book "Kichhi hasa, Kichhita Bidrup" published by Granth Mandir, Cuttack. It may be possible in a few days.

1988-1992 – Many satirical stories translated to Hindi were published in Hindi weekly magazines.

2001- one of his English books "Shiridi Sai Baba and other Perfect Masters" has been published by Sterling Publications, New Delhi. This book is already translated into Hindi, Marathi, Tamil, Telgu, Odia, Bangali and Gujurati Languages. This book is also available in Ukranian and Nepali Languages.

2004 – An Odia book containing various devotional Songs, "Bhakti Naibedya" was published by the Sadhana Thust.

2005 – One Hindi book "Sai Sharan me" was also published by the Sterling Publications. A lot of devotional and Sai bhakti-related songs are available in this.

2009 – The English book of Guruji, "Baba May I Answer" is published by the Sterling publications, New Delhi and are available in all Sai temples. This book is also translated in to Hindi, Marathi, Telgu, Odia, Bengli and Gujurati languages.

2010 – He has written an Odia book based on the science of the world and the origin of the world. The name of the book is "Gopya ru Agopya". The entire book is written in fourteen letter verses. This book was launched by Hon'ble Governor of Odisha, Shri Muralidhar Chandrakanta Bhandare, in the presence of eminent writers of Odisha, Chancellors of different Universities of Odisha, Sanskrit professors, Sanskrit scholars and many learned persons of Odisha. Later the Sanskrit version of this book was also inaugurated.

During 5th January 2012 to 10th January 2012, the World Sanskrit Conference was held at Vigyan Bhaban, New Delhi. The Prime Minister of India presided over it. On this occasion, his book "Srusthi Tatwanuchintanan" was highly appreciated by the representatives from many countries of the world.

2010-2011 – written in Odia in Nabakhyari Chhand, Shri Guru Bhagabat (First, second, third, fourth and fifth part) is an unique achievement in Odia Literature. The author of this book is Shri Chandra Bhanu Satpathy and this is available in the market since 2011. This valuable book is a literary creation where importance of all (Guru, disciple and general public) is described. This book is a religions book containing about 16,000 lines. Many parts of this book have been aired on Radio and TV channels. Not only the Odia people, but also the non-Odia people are reading this book and feeling its essence. Now the first and second part of this book has already been printed in English and Hindi.

2012 – A Hindi book "Sai Sumiran me" and "Sri Sai Smarane" in Odia has already been printed. The books are loaded with devotional songs and hymns.

From 1993 till today – Guruji Satpathy is the patron of many religious magazines like Sai Ananta (Marathi), Sai heritage (English), Sai Darshan (Hindi), Sai Bani (Odia), Sai Kirnalu (Telgu) and Sai Krupa (Hindi).

2013 – The fifth part of Shri Guru bhagabat was offered to Sai Baba. Four parts were already released. Now the fifth part is also available in all Sai temples.

2013 – "Shri Sai Satcharitra" and "Shri Sai Aradhana" books were unveiled. These books are now available in all the Sai temples.

THE INVOLVEMENT OF SHRI CHANDRA BHANU SATPATHY IN THE CULTURAL SPHERE

In 2011, Guruji was presented with "Baidyanath Sangeeta Ratna Puraskar" by Tapasya Sangeet Academy, Deoghar in Tharkhand. This award is given for excellence in music.

On 4th November 2011, he was honoured with the title of "Divya Sangeet Shiromani" by Shri Shiridi Sai Baba Cultural Trust at Bhubaneswar, Odisha. This title is generally given to the composers of devotional songs and composer of various tunes.

THE CONTRIBUTION OF GURUJI TO MUSIC

He is well known in Akashbani centre as a composer of Gajals, Bhajans etc. in Hindi since 1983. Shri Chandra Bhanu Satpathy, the composer of devotional music, helped to make cassettes in both Hindi and Odia. He himself did both the composition and lyrics of each song (Hindi, Odia and other languages). Cassettes and CDs of his composition are now available in all Sai temples.

In 2009, "Times Music", Mumbai released a C.D. in which the writings and vocal co-ordinations of Guruji had taken place. The name of the C.D. was "Living with Sai". All these devotional songs were sung by Leading Singers of Bollywood. They were Suresh Wadekar, Sadhana Saragam, Shankar Mahadevan, Sukhabindar Singh and Silpa Rao. "Times Music" of Mumbai had released another C.D. in 2010. Shri Satpathy himself had donated his voice in this C.D. The title of this C.D. was "Aao Sai". These devotional songs have been sung by renowned Singers like Shreya Ghosal, Rekha Bharadwaj, Shan, Shankar Mahadevm, Kailash Kher and Shilpa Rao.

In 2011 Guruji Shri Satpathy had prepared a devotional C.D. in H.M.V. Saregama Institute, Kolkata, whose writer, composer was he himself. The name of the C.D. was "Shri Sainathay Namoh Namoh". In 2011, two Odia C.D.s were prepared by Shri Satpathy. The first one was "Shri Guru Bhagabat and Shri Jagannath Stabak" and the second was "Shri Sai Charane". He had written these hymns. In this year, the first part of Guru Bhagabat was published in three volumes.

A C.D named "Shri Jagannathay Namah" was prepared by the H.M.V. Saregama, Kolkata, which contains many devotional songs written by Guruji. In 2012, a C.D. prepared with all the writings of the book "Gopya ru Agopya" was also available.

A festival is being held every year on Basanta Panchami

i.e. Saraswati Puja at Sai Mandir in Gurugaon under the patronage of Guruji. Guruji Shri Chandra Bhanu Satpathy is the priest of the festival. People who are excellent in dance and music participate in the festival. The people among them are Padmasri Birju Maharaj (Kathak dance), Padma Bivusan Ustad Sabrikhan, Geeta Mahalik (Odishi dance), Ajit Kadkade, Mumbai (Religious Songs) etc. Many artists of Mayurbhanj Chhau dance were also felicitated.

RELIGIOUS AND SPIRITUAL PROGRAMMES

The "Sai Prerana" trust of Mumbai had congratulated Shriman Chandra Bhanu Satpathy for miraculously spreading the glory of Shiridi Sai Baba to every corner of the world. This programme was prepared by both "Sai Prerana" and "Star TV". On this occasion, a devotional music programme "Mallik ek Sura Anek" was telecasted by the Star TV. Film actor Shri Bibek Oberoi had also congratulated Guruji there. Many singers, actors and other artists of the Hindi film world like Jacky Shrof, Kajol, Tanuja, Suresh Wadekar and Shriya Ghoshal etc. participated in this programme.

The Odia Society of America, Plano in Texas had congratulated Shriman Satpathy in their annual function (July 2011). This Society is formed in Plano city in Texas State of America. This felicitation was accorded to him for his spiritual and divine knowledge. Apart from it, he was also felicitated by various Indian institutions for his dedication to human services and his expertise in music and literature.

On 8th April 2012, he was decorated with the first "Prarthana Samman" award by the Prarthana TV channel. This TV channel of Odisha preaches devotional music and knowledge related to various spiritual consciousnesses.

Shriman Chandra Bhanu Satpathy has a library of his own, where different journals, valuable English books and Odia writings (some are hand-written) are kept carefully. This is conducive to research work. There are around 3000 books and writings in the Library and this number is growing gradually. It is Guruji's opinion that this library will be helpful for researching on Shiridi Sai Baba. Many writings and books on Baba are available in this library for any research work.

THE SAI MOVEMENT IN INDIA

In 1989, Shriman Chandra Bhanu Satpathy became a devotee of Shiridi Sai Baba. Sai Baba is the famous Sidha Purush of Maharashtra whose blessings has inspired Shri Chandra Bhanu Satpathy to spread Sai fame. Guruji Satpathy is the only devotee who has expanded the idea of Sai Baba in different parts of the world. Today Sai temples are visible in different parts of India. Lakhs of people of our country and abroad are following the path prescribed by Baba. On the guidance of Guruji Satpathy, more than 300 Sai temples are established in every nook and corner of the world. He also served as the chief patron of more than 60 spiritual and charitable institutions.

Shriman Satpathy had arranged many camps on Sai Baba in different Kumbha Melas (Allahabad - 1995, 2001, 2007, Nasik-2003, Haridwar-2004) and also in Tigri Mela at Garh Mukteswar on the banks of Ganges. This place is within Meerut and Moradabad districts. Thousands of Sai devotees attended and received Baba's Blessings and divine teachings. Shri Satpathy is a leading person to initiate camps on various issues of Sai Baba. He had decided to open a Sai stall at Puri at the time of Jagannath Car festival and ultimately fixed the stall by bringing books, portraits etc. from different places of Odisha. This activity is continuing since 2002.

He also tried to build 30 Hindu temples and succeeded.

INTERNATIONAL SAI MOVEMENT

Sai festivals (International conference on Shiridi Sai Baba) have been organised in various countries (Chicago - 2001; America - 2009, Sidney - 2002, Canada, U.K. and South Africa - 2001) by the efforts of Shriman Satpathy. More than ten temples have been built due to sincere endeavour of Guruji in countries like U.S.A., Australia, U.K. and South Africa.

Guruji Shri Satpathy has delivered many speeches on TV and radio in Chicago, Dallas (U.S.A.), Johannesburg (South Africa) and some other countries. He also explained to the people about Sai Baba's fame and the peace one gets when they come in contact with Him.

OTHER FAMES

On 11th July 2008, the North Odisha University had felicitated Shriman Satpathy as "Mayurbhanjar Khyati Samparna Balak". In 2011, the "Odia Pua" organisation of New Delhi had accorded the title "Odia Ratna" to him. This title is generally given to any Odia person for his contribution in the field of music, Literature, Social Services and spiritual matters.

The Odia people living in Dallas, America asked Guruji to say something in a meeting. He delivered a summarising lecture on various religious principles to the people of America. After the speech, Professor Digambar Mishra, Shri Jagannath Rath and Shri Hara Patra, on behalf of this Society, had felicitated Guruji in view of his selfless service, spiritual outlook and literary expertise.

on 27th September 2012, the Seattle Cultural Centre (Washington) had awarded the "Building bridges across nation" award to Guruji. This Cultural centre gives this award for humane ideas of human beings. Guruji is the first Indian to get this award.

In the year 2012, the Utkal Sahitya Samaj, Cuttack had honoured Guruji with the "Govind Narayan Adhyatmik Sahitya Samman" award for his great contribution to Odia Literature.

Whenever Guruji visits Bhubaneswar, some cultural functions are arranged. Its main purpose is that all Sai Lovers will come in contact with Guruji. Along with it, temple establishment programmes, interaction of Sai devotees with Guruji, review of various temple issues etc. are also discussed. His advice is the most important thing. I came to know that some of the devotees who have worked without taking his advice have faced many difficulties. Therefore, I request the Sai devotees to inform Guruji about their problems, however simple it may be.

Respecting Guru is not a new thing. This honouring has been continuing since long. In some Schools, worshiping Guru with Sandalwood paste and flowers is common. No Guru divas is celebrated for college teachers. Only that day is declared as holiday. Many teachers and Lecturers are respected by me and due to the blessings of them, I was able to serve in the university for 20 years as a professor. I believe it was the blessings of my teachers that pulled me this far. It is the Guru's blessings which do good to all of us.

Even though Shri Chandra Bhanu Satpathy is

younger than me, I have given him the place of Guru. My other Guru is Prof. Pranakrushna Parija. He is a soft spoken person. He does not take any problem seriously. I have never seen a person like him who oversees an experiment so diligently. I may have learnt from him how to look at slides under a microscope and express my opinion. The main purpose of a research is to see something new and that requires a lot of efforts.

I know Prof. Parija as the Chancellor. But his vast knowledge of the new principles of Botany at his advanced age astonished me. Another good quality of Parija Saheb was punctuality. If he said that he will reach the Laboratory at 9 O'clock then his car will reach the gate exactly at 9 O'clock. If unable to reach by 9 O'clock then he will inform it by telephone. But this situation has never happened with me. I have written an article in Odia "Ame Swapna Kahinki Dekhu?" (Why do we dream?) which was published in 1957. The article may have been good but I later thought that there was something wrong with the language. In 1958, I got a Job at Ravenshaw College and devoted a lot of time to teach in one or two departments of Botany. I have almost stopped writing Odia articles. Now whatever I am writing in Odia, these are on Sai Baba only. My inner feeling indicates that Sai Baba is helping me a lot in writing all this.

I came in contact with many Odia Lecturers when I was Deputy Registrar in Sambalpur University (1967 to 1971). They also gave me some of their articles to read. Most of the times, I read those writings and tried to understand them. This effort may be helping me to write in Odia. The purpose of writing all this is that now the people (students, teachers or office staffs) are proud of not knowing their mother tongue and consider themselves to be the most powerful and respectful people in the society by speaking English and using that Language in their daily work. There are some people who use 50% English words in their Odia speaking. One may be speaking English words involuntarily from his own speech. One tries his best to speak pure Odia but while speaking, some English words such as building, road, over bridge, construction and many other words get mixed.

THE ARRIVAL OF SAIBABA IN GURUJI SHRI CHANDRA BHANU SATPATHY'S LIFE AND OTHER SADGURUS

Guruji Shri Satpathy first came to know about Sai Baba's miracles from a cassette. That cassette was full of many miracle incidents. Perhaps he had got his first intimacy with Baba from this Cassette. Among many miraculous happenings of Baba, the incident of Baba passing in to Samadhi, that too for 72 hours, had greatly amazed him. After this incident, a picture of Guruji's father appeared in that place. He started watching this incident repeatedly on the TV Screen. He could not understand the reason behind it. He did not understand at all the connections between seeing his father's picture on the TV screen again and again, viewing the scene of Baba's Samadhi and the passionate prayers of devotees.

Guruji Satpathy first went to Muktidham in Nasik. Muktidham is a large multi-sectioned temple that can accommodate 200 devotees at a time. In that temple there were many deities as well as a seated statue of Baba sitting on a stone. A fiery and lovely idol to behold. It was a wish of Guruji to garland the statue. Truly, the priest asked Guruji to put the garland on the idol. He did not expect this surprising event but he had a tremendous desire in the heart to do it. Usually, the garland is removed after putting on a new one. But in this case it was not like that and it remained on Baba's body. Placing the garland may be accidental but the garland remaining on Baba's body is very surprising. Praying on this matter may have been the divine directive from Baba or it may be a sign of receiving the garland due to invoking Baba mentally. However, the experience of offering this garland was remembered by Guruji forever. It may be a common coincidence or some divine signal, only Sai Baba could know.

He had felt that Sai Baba sent a message to him that the agony of not getting a signal has already ended. Of course, understanding it in the judgment of the intellect is a different matter. But the feeling of opening the door of the universe for him drowned him in an ocean of inexhaustible joy. Even with such hints, the game of intelligence in the form of doubts and questions continued.

On that day, he reached Shiridi at about 12 o'clock noon. That was Thursday and there was a stream of devotees. Thursday is an auspicious day and it is Baba's day. He felt himself Lucky to have gone to see Baba on that day. The line moved slowly forward. Hardly he had advanced a short distance, when he remembered about his air travel. Such speed of line may not conducive to his flight timing. There will be a lot of trouble if the flight will be missed. So many thoughts like this started circulating in his mind. In that situation, it may be impossible to do anything except praying. He was praying desperately. After some time some one offered to arrange for his early darsan (seeing the deities). That gentleman has seen him many times in Delhi but he does not remember. He went in and returned shortly after talking with someone and led them all through a house to the "Samadhi Pithastha" (Tomb). The very sight of Baba's face caused an indescribable joy in Guruji's mind and heart, which he had never felt before.

He did not seem to know when the garland had fallen on the Samadhi Pitha (Tomb) after darsan. Perhaps his consciousness is his spiritual experience of emptiness and union. He was not able to know when the priest has put the garland on the tomb. Now a days, wreaths are placed on the Samadhi (Tomb). We learned that this practice will also be stopped after a few days.

By the time they came out of the temple and visited Khandoba temple, Dwaraka Mai and sat under Neem trees, it was almost 2 PM. They heard that there was no food available in Langer (community kitchen). He thought that if only a little Khiri (Rice boiled with milk) would be available, then his mind would calm down to some extent. Because, the food can be available in outside hotels but the Khiri of Baba will not. A Sebak (servant) of Sai institute came and informed him that the food would be served in the VIP room. After waiting for some time, the person who said that all the food will be available, suddenly came and said that all the food is finished and apologised for it. But he assured to arrange some Khiri. Actually, Guruji had prayed Baba for a little Khiri only. Perhaps as a result of this prayer, Khiri was available for all. Call it coincidence or Baba's infinite mercy, his idea that it was no coincidence became stronger and tears began to flow from his eyes. Here Guruji said that he finally found his lost spiritual master. Sai Baba also did not come straight to him but was able to pull him towards him by twisting and turning.

Guruji wrote that Sainath had performed a Leela during his lifetime and now what he is doing without a body is another Leela. "Om Shri Sainathay Namah" - He used to recite this mantra in his mind again and again. He started visiting the Sai temple at Lodhi road, Delhi almost every day. By 1990s, the number of people coming to see him grew unexpectedly. Before coming in contact with Sai Baba, Guruji used to conduct experiments on people by using pyramids. But on the top of all this only the idea that "Sainam is the best method" was born. Not only idea but it came as a reality. Due to his constant meditation on Shri Sainath he was entering into a strange world. Many people say that Sai Baba has ordered them to meet him. It is not only Delhi but people who have come to visit him from different parts of India also say that Sai Baba has commanded them to do so. No matter how much he refused, the number of people was not coming down. They were convinced that he possessed supernatural powers.

The solution to all problems is to pray Shri Sainath. Guruji has solved many amazing critical problems by praying deeply to Sai Baba. As per the Language of Sai, one endures the fruits of his actions not only in the next birth, but also in this life.

Here, I am presenting an amazing story. How painful is the quarrel between father and mother on the minds of children and as a result they decide to leave the house. One such incident had happened in Delhi where three sons left their house because they could not bear the quarrel between their father and mother. Their whereabouts could not be ascertained despite intensive searching. Guruji prayed before Sainath for the solution of this problem. As if, those three children appeared in his vision. One of the three was walking with a limp. Guruji advised those two persons to worship at Sai temple on Lodhi Road. He also asked them to cover the shrine with Yellow cloth. Of course, Baba has no interest in all this. Only surrender to Sai is enough. Guruji and others (including father and mother of the children) prayed to Sai Baba for those children. Wonder of wonders ! After two days they got a phone call informing them that their children were safe there. One leg of a child has been injured. Since that day, Sai Baba has been worshiped in their house.

Many people come to Guruji for advice, only to guide their personal life. Many letters started coming to Guruji from people from different sections of the society and different communities. Guruji had only one medicine to cure all these pains i.e. "Sai Naam". Sai Baba is full of compassion. Whether it is sickness or pain, everything will be cured if we will pray Him. There is no doubt about it. Guruji often used to send Bibhuti (udi) and photos of Sai Baba. The experiences and happenings of the families to whom the bibhuti (udi) and photos were sent were more amazing and extraordinary. At the root of all supernatural events was Sai Ram. This name is the medicine for all the diseases.

The number of people coming to Guruji gradually increased as he has received the spiritual nourishment from Shri Sai. The greater the scarcity, the greater is the pain, suffering and greed. Many times, most of the people are just chasing worldly happiness with inconsistent desires and dishonest means.

No medicine or no intellectual advice can solve this problem. For them Sai Baba is the only medicine, which he continues to dispense till this day. Guruji observed that Sainam is the best method by which many people can overcome many of their losses and problems.

He started meditating on Shri Sainath and as a result he wandered in a strange world. Whether it was because of his meditation or because of some divine directions, the number of devotees began to increase day by day. These devotees usually said that it was an order through a dream. But Guruji was telling them to refrain from it. But it was seen that this number continued to increase day after day. These people were explaining that they had received strange instructions to meet. Guruji wrote that despite many denials, more and more people were coming to meet him by the instruction of a divine power. They believed that Guruji must have some divine power that was dragging them to him. May be there is some attraction that draws people towards him. He thought that these supernatural phenomena were all coincidences, no doubt about it. In London, he wrote, an elderly woman could not walk but could only get around on a stretcher. By the Blessings of Sai Baba, she was able to walk slowly by drinking udi mixed water and applying a little on her body. Now she does not feel any pain in visiting Shiridi and viewing Baba.

Guruji Satpathy read all the books written by Meher Baba and Upasani Maharaj and started meditation on Sai Nath to solve his many questions. As a result of this process, he found his answers. Perhaps, it was this belief of Guruji that he could see the answers to all the questions in his mind and the answers were so clear that as if, they were already decided. Now Let's see that those who come to visit Guruji are just to pay their respects to him or they have some problems or difficulties which they do not have any solutions.

The fame of Guruji grew day after day. The newspapers have played a huge role in this rise in popularity. As a result of this, the crowds started increasing day-by-day. Many respected people, business men, politicians and administrators started coming to Guruji. The purpose of their visit was to solve their worldly problems. They had full faith that only Guruji could solve all these problems. Among these people, there were also some who had already left their families. It must be a surprising event which is difficult to him to comprehend. He was always thinking, why such type of people are coming to him? Does he have the ability to see the spiritual path? There was nothing, no training, no basis of knowledge and no attitude. In fact, God's will is very strange. It is also difficult to know His intentions. He came to know that many people had heartwarming experiences. Some of them were of the supernatural level and Sai Baba was also of the supernatural level and all the events during his lifetime were visible. So there was no problem in knowing the results - many supernatural events are still happening.

A young businessman, an ardent devotee of Sai Nath, lost his son who suffered from Down syndrome disease. Even after that, he did not lose faith and hope on Baba. Before incinerating his son's dead body in the pyre, he placed Sai's amulet around his son's neck and prayed deeply to Sai Nath for his son's return once again. Despite such a big blow, he did not lose faith in Baba.

A few days later Anil's wife became pregnant once again and he and his wife got themselves tested to know if they have any symptoms of this disease. The medical examination revealed that the symptoms of the disease exist with them. So there was no other way but only to pray to Baba. Two days after the child's birth medical tests revealed that the boy was free from any type of chromosomal disorder. A mole mark appeared on the body of the new born son, on the same place exactly where the mole was on the dead son's body. It was also of the same colour and shape. This was possible only due to unwavering faith in Baba. Could we develop such a faith?

Many miracles happened during the life time of Baba, which are difficult to describe. Like Anil, many incidents came to the people's attention and some incidents do not come to the lime light. It is difficult to record whatever is coming: Baba has not disappointed the devotee who wants to have Him with a pure heart. Guruji wrote, "How does Baba get so much time to solve so many problems ?" It is really beyond the boundary of our knowledge.

THE MYSTERIOUS LIFE OF SAI

The early life of Sai Baba is shrouded in mystery. His birth, father's identity, place of birth, childhood, and childhood education are also shrouded with mystery. Since these things are still mysteries there is no authentic proof about them, so they should be treated as fiction. Being fictions, some of them contradict with each other. Therefore, their credibility and acceptability remain in doubt. Baba also did not answer any questions related to his father's identity and his early life.

Once a thief was caught by the police with all the stolen goods and the police recovered them from him. When asked, he clarified that all those things were given by Baba and he get them from him. At that time, Baba's fame had spread all around and he had a large following of devotees. So, no one should give importance to such a complaint. But the Dhulia court appointed a pleader Commission to exonerate Baba from the taint of the charges. Its main purpose was to free

Baba from this complaint. Apart from it, examining him who is the source of all the spiritual powers and has assumed a form is a symbol of materialism. Despite all these, Baba agreed to cooperate with the Commissioner.

Such a situation had arisen in the case of the great Sufi saint Hazrat Nizamuddin Auliya. The Ulemas who were openly jealous of the Saint, made serious complaints against him to the Sultan. As a result, there was an order from the Sultan that Hazrat himself would be present and answer the Complaint. Of course, there was no need for him to be present himself. It was impossible on the part of the Sultan to present him forcibly, by using the Scepter, in his court as he was in possession of great spiritual power. Still, Hazrat Saheb had decided to reach the Sultan's court. Because, he had thought that if he remained absent, it would be a disobedience to the Sultan's orders and a severe blow to the Royal power. He also did not want to weaken the royal power. Likewise, Sai Baba also agreed to appear before the court appointed Commissioner to answer the questions.

When the Commissioner questioned him about the identity of his parents, Shri Sainath answered, Brahma is my father and Maya is my mother.

This entire universe is created due to the union of Brahma and Maya. It is eternal and even new. By this Sai indicated that he was a part of Brahma. This could mean that Sai did not take birth like others. He was really unborn or not born from mother's womb.

He assumed the human body to fulfill a special purpose. His demise is also covered with mystery. Perhaps he never left his body. Who knows, there may be nothing left in his grave.

In the past, conflicts arose between the Hindu and Muslim devotees of Kabir as they wanted to cremate his body according to their own religious beliefs. But when the shroud was removed from Kabir's body, surprisingly only some flowers remained there. They divided the flowers among themselves and the disciples of both the communities performed his last rites according to their own traditions. As per the authentic information recorded in the village register, it was found that the thief took the Shelter of lie to implicate Baba. Baba was not giving specific answers to all the questions. It was beyond the reach of an ordinary judge to understand the mystery of his answers or to draw a conclusion from it.

Here are some of the popular theories collected by Guruji Satpathy regarding Baba's appearance on this world. He said and also admitted that such works are purely speculation and he has not done any analysis on it. He has written those theories as they have evolved periodically in the course of time. Given below are some of the theories-

A) Mhalsapathi was one of the close devotees of Baba. He served Baba with great devotion and used to sleep with Him in Dwarakamai. One night Baba told Mhalsapathi the secret of his birth. The devotees from Parthi kept coming to Baba regularly and Baba also used to ask them about the residents of the village. It is believed that the said Fakir was a Sufi Saint and the Guru of Baba. Baba had spent many years with him during his childhood. Baba had an unwavering devotion towards his Guru and was always eloquent in praise of him. The story of his devotion to his Guru is found in many folk tales and folk songs.

B) It is mentioned in another book that Shri Sai Nath

was born in Parthi village situated on the bank of Godavari River. His parents were very religious but childless at first. By the grace of Shiva, the couple had Sai Nath as their son. But as they had already renounced the world, they surrendered the boy to the God and left. Abandoned by his parents under a tree in the forest, the child was accidentally spotted by a passing Fakir and his wife. They were overjoyed by it. But as a teenager, Sai had no attachment to worldly affairs. He always continued to worship only to Lord Shiva with deep devotion. In the result, the Fakir became angry and threw Sai Nath out of his house. Sai, the boy, wandered as a hermit and finally reached Shiridi.

C) Das Ganu Maharaj was one of the closest disciples of Baba. He had gone to Shridi with the arrogance of a policeman to examine Baba but the result was just reverse. Instead of exposing Baba by examining him, he had exposed himself. He surrendered himself to the divine power of Baba and identified himself as one of his chief disciples. He composed such devotional songs and dohas describing Baba's name and fame that they were sung in all homes of Maharashtra. Like Mardana, the disciple of Guru Nanak, Das Ganu sheds some light on Baba's early life in his tome "Bhakti Sarimrut".

In the village of Jambawar in Maharashtra, there lived a devotee of Lord Venkateswar named Keshav Rao. As he was childless, he prayed to Venkateshu (Vishnu) for a son. In a dream Lord Vishnu gave him the boon that Swami Ramananda of Kashi would be born as his son. A son was born to Keshav Rao in time. From the very beginning this strange boy began to show signs of deep piety and devotion. His father got him married to stimulate attraction towards the worldly affairs. But he had no interest in these earthly things. He was donating food, clothes and money to the poor, helpless people within his limited resources. But this limited donation could not give him satisfaction. Therefore, he left the house and went to Salar (Melawadi) in Maharashtra and lived there. Through his hard work and his own virtues, he gradually rose in the ranks and in time was recognised as a Jagirdar under the regime Nizam. The people more affectionately called him as Jamidar Gopal Rao.

Jamidar Gopal Rao was the most generous man. He distributed the zamidari revenue among the needy and poor, which helped them to eliminate their poverty. Gradually this work gave him various celestial powers. He was able to restore the sight of a blind woman by applying chilli powder in a strange way. Many people were cured by his extraordinary treatment. While paying his devotional respect at the dargah of Sufi Saint Suhag Sah located in Ahmed Nagar, he heard a grave divine voice from inside the dargah. "Your disciple Kabir will appear ten miles away from the city of Manmath, as the son of a Fakir. Again he heard that, he himself was Ramananda, the guru of Kabir in his last birth." In the end, the responsibilities of Kabir rested on Jamidar Gopal Rao. A few days after this incident the Fakir's widow came to meet Gopal Rao with a five year old boy. When the boy was 12 years old, his mother died and he became lonely. A heavenly relationship developed between the boy and Gopal Rao. Once these two had gone to deep forest and did not return for four months. Gopal Rao's family, out of jealousy, blamed the boy for leaving the house of Gopal Rao. Fueled by hatred and vengeance, they set out to find the two in the forest. When they saw both of them sitting under a tree, they pelted the boy with bricks and stones. A brick hit Gopal Rao on his head instead of hitting the boy and blood flowed from that impacted place. The bleeding was stopped by tying it with a cloth. Seeing Guru's condition, the boy was so sad that he blamed himself as the cause of Guru's misfortune. He appealed to the Guru to go away. The reply of the Guru was, "My final hour has reached, so today I will hand over everything to you and leave". He instructed the boy to collect some milk from a black cow. A black cow was found but there was no milk in the udder but as soon as the guru touched the udder of the Cow, milk started pouring out. He asked to collect three Sers of milk. The internal meaning of three Sers of milk is Karma, devotion and wisdom.

After taking the milk, the disciple feels a divine transformation inside him. He saw Narayan everywhere. That divine form of Narayan filled the earth and sky and spread throughout the entire universe. Guru reminded him that "You are Kabir. You have taken rebirth. In the previous birth you had followed a family life, in this birth you will lead a life of total celibacy and will observe the vow of silence. You stay in one place only and ascend the consciousness of devotees who surrender completely to you. Now I will leave for that place and dissolve there in my Mahasamadhi."

Saying this, he removed the bandaged cloth from his head and tied it around the head of his disciple. That piece of brick and that piece of cloth were kept carefully by the disciple as a memento of the Guru till the end of his life.

After that, a strange thing happened. The person who cracked the head of the Guru by throwing the brick, died suddenly. The awareness of the people, who were pursuing, arose at last. They prayed at the Guru's feet to forgive all the sins of the deceased and bring him back to life. But the Guru said that he had already transferred all his divine powers to his disciple. So he cannot do anything himself. Therefore, there was no other way but to request the disciple. The guru instructed the boy Sai to revive the dead. After taking a little clay from the Guru's feet and applying it on the dead man's forehead, the dead man came back to life. He fell at the Guru's feet and apologised for his impudence. The public was totally dumb founded. It was beyond their imagination that the dead could come back to life. Of course, it can be taken as the last stage of divine power. Because, in it the Law of nature is not only controlled, it also has to rise above it. So, praising the noble deeds of master and disciple, they took them in a procession and set off to selu. The next day the Guru entered into his Mahasamadhi. Dressed in a Kafani, the disciple went to the south bank of river Godavari and finally took Shiridi as his place of work. This boy was none other than Sai Nath.

D) Sivamma (103 year old) was a devotee of Shri Sainath. For about fifteen years before attaining Shri Sainath's Mahasamadhi, Sivamma used to come to Shiridi intermittently and engaged herself in His Service. What she has written about Shri Sainath's childhood is given below.

Shri Sai Nath was born as the son of a brahmin couple named Vithal and Chakrapani Amma. Many children of the couple who were born before Shri Sai were not survived. While Shri Sai Nath was still in his mother's womb, the couple were travelling in a forest under the Nizam of Hyderabad regime, when the labor pain of his mother started. An unprecedented heavenly child was born in a nearby cowshed. Right after his birth, a Fakir came and said "This child is not an ordinary child, he is destined to become the Guru of all the living beings of the world." He is an incarnation of God. After three months, I will come to this place and take him with me.

Exactly three months later, the Fakir arrived at the place and took the child named Babu with him from the distressed parents. He was brought up with utmost care by the Fakir and his wife and when he was five-year-old, the Fakir requested his wife to offer him to Venkusha who was a devotee of Balajee and residing in Selu village. Meanwhile, God himself appeared in a dream and said to Venkusha - I am coming in a boy's form to be your disciple. This boy was Kabir Das in his previous birth. The next day, Fakir's wife came to Venkusha with the boy. Venkusha's body turned to ice as soon as he saw the boy and it became still and motionless. After calling Kabir Das, Kabir Das three times, his life energy returned.

Venkusha loved Baba the most among all his disciples. This created jealousy among others. One day, while Baba and Venkusha were meditating, a jealous disciple threw a brick at Baba - Baba immediately raised his hand. As a result the brick hung in the air.

Venkusha asked Baba to bring the piece of Brick. On the instruction of the Guru Baba brought that piece of brick and kept it himself. Guru's directive was "when this brick will be broken, then you will know that it is time to take your Samadhi." This was the prediction of the Guru. After that he asked Baba to bring some cow milk and blessed him and said "you should preach this principle in the society that there is no difference between the human beings." Our duty is to be kind, compassionate and loving to all. Finally the Guru Shri Venkusha blessed and said that a devotee who bows down before Baba's picture or portrait will never face any scarcity of anything.

The boy who threw the brick suddenly fell dead. Seeing this, all his friends realised their mistake and requested Guru Venkusha to revive the dead child. On the instruction of the Guru, Shri Sainath gave him life.

E) Baba always used a brick as a pillow. Baba has told many times to Nana Saheb Chandorkar that the brick was given by his Guru.

When this brick will be broken, then you will know that the day has come for me to leave this world. This is the same brick that my Gurudev endured by putting his head before it and saved my life. Just before Baba's Maha Samadhi the brick fell from the hands of the boy who was always cleaning the Dwarakamayi and broken into two pieces. Seeing this, Baba cried out "it indicates that the time has reached to leave my body." After sometime of this incident, he immersed in Maha Samadhi.

F) Shri Sai Sharmananda Swami has given an account of Baba's childhood life. Swamiji has written in the article that Shri Sai Nath left his own parents and came to the banks of the Ganges. He left for Shiridi and had the darsan of his Guru. The name of his Guru was Shah Rosan Mian. Sai Baba served him for twelve years with unwavering devotion.

Being satisfied with his devotion, the Guru had bestowed him with the boom - I will always protect you, no matter where you are, whether here or in another kingdom across the seven oceans. As a sacrificial fee, the Guru asked for two things, Shradha (full faith) and Saburi (patience). These two are the prime principles of Sai marga.

I knowingly refrain myself from presenting my own theory about Baba's birth and childhood. It is such a mystery that no one can reveal it correctly or certainly. It is a heavenly mystery because Sai himself was a heavenly messenger. There are still spiritual seekers who are constantly in contact with Sai. But this is not a mystery for them at all. Baba knew that man is divided into two parts. One part worships the physical form of the God and the other part worships the incorporeal God. Therefore, he has permitted his devotees to worship him with both the views. While in Shirdi, his devotees not only saw him as their own deity Shri Ram or Shri Krishna, but also saw Baba as their own Guru. Every day, many years after he had left his earthly body, some disciples have had the privilege of seeing him in person. He had assumed the physical form to fulfill a special purpose of the God. Baba descended to earth for those devotees who could not come close to him mentally.

There was no need for Sai Baba to take birth from a mother's womb. Who knows, he might be a Ajoni Sambhut (not born from a woman's reproductive system). Jesus Christ was born from Mary, the symbol of virginity. Shri Sai is of that level. One could only follow the path shown by Sai within their respective religion.

Love is the symbol of Sai. The heavenly Love which could envelop all the living beings of this world has no Limit, no obstacle, no rise and no fall, which is not limited and where there is no dullness or confusion. This Love which is spread everywhere in this world is the symbol of the universal consciousness. Simplicity and extreme self sacrificing is his life, which is impossible for any ordinary human being to observe. This is the same Sai whose origin we are researching continuously. Godliness has neither a beginning nor an end. So, what is the point of debating this? Is not it more appropriate to discuss how Jesus Christ laughingly endured death to save the suffering and helpless men than to waste time on a futile intellectual exercise of how he was born from the virgin Marry? Is not it enough to know that during his life time and even after giving up his life, this saintly man had saved countless people by his guidance?

Is Sai still not doing it ? If in Sai's version, he has no beginning or no ending and is always a part of the creation, then the question arises, what was before the creation ? Its answer is the great void and the eternal man. In the eternal flow of time, the eternal man is the divine being. At His direction many universes are born and dissolved. He is the source of the eternal flow of the creation. Sai is that great void and the creator (Adi Purush). How do we know the source of his emergence ? Even the vedas are also silent in this regard. So it is pointless to make any assumptions about it.

Sai Baba of Shiridi had stayed in Shiridi for about sixty years (1858 to 1918). When he came permanently to Shiridi, the name of God was always in his mind and he was so absorbed in it that he did not know anything about the society and he had no sense of time. He always sat in meditation under a neem tree. He loved very much to stay alone. A village women named Bayaji, out of compassion, used to search Baba in different places and forced him to eat. Baba suddenly left for four years (i.e. from 1854 to 1858) and returned again in the year 1858. No one knows anything about where he was and what he was doing during these four years.

His actual place of birth, name of the family etc. are a

total mystery. However, some researchers speculate that Baba was born in the village Prarthi in Maharastra between 1835 and 1838 AD. Whether he was a Hindu or Muslim is not known clearly till now. Because Baba did not show any interest on any questions regarding the matter. He kept his beard and mustache. He wore a long robe (Alkhala) and a cloth (Patka) tied on his head like the Sufis, but also pierced his ears like the Hindus. He could talk in Urdu, Hindi, Marathi and some South Indian languages. He used to participate in the functions of both Hindus and Muslims. In short, his religion was universal brotherhood and humanism. After his second visit to Shiridi, he spent sixty years in a dilapidated mosque. However, he used to stay some nights in another nearby place called Chavadi. Fakirs, Sufi Saints and Hindu sages were coming to him regularly. To beg from some houses in Shiridi was the part of his daily life and he was distributing the foods received by begging to the animals, birds and poor people. He used to treat the people with a kind of herbal medicine. At first the local Hindu community looked upon him with suspicion, but when they benefited from the divine power of this benevolent Fakir, the situation changed dramatically. A farmer named Tatya Kote Patil, Goldsmith Mhalsapathi, School teacher Shyama, Police employee Das Ganu, Magistrate Nama Saheb Chondarkar, the Millionaire from Nagpur Utmarna Buti, Advocate from Bombay Kaka Saheb Dixit, Abdul and hundreds of established people from different walks of life from far and wide places began to gather around him. All of them not only gained knowledge, but also gained comfort. They also received worldly and supernatural help. Gradually his name spread to different parts of India and everyday hundred of devotees started coming to Shiridi, like visiting temples.

Gradually, many people came in contact with Sai and his fame spread widely. Many devotional songs were also written. As if, Dwarakamayi Masjid was seemed like a royal court. Those who came never returned disappointed.

Shri Sai always kept the Masjid very clean. He restored all the dilapidated temples. He also planted trees and took care of them. The garden he created is known today as the Lendi Bag garden. He was able to create an atmosphere of mutual respect and cooperation in all the departments of social life. To establish unity among all the devotees, he himself attended all religions festivals and promoted group prayers and mass meals. With the help of devotees, he built three rest houses. They were called "Wada" and named as Sathe wada, Buti wada and Dixit wada. They were built for staying and resting of the devotees. From time to time, Shri Sai would feed the devotees with food cooked by himself and used to cure their ailments by providing the bibhuti (udi) from his Dhuni (fire). The place of his Dhuni was called Dwarakamayi. This tradition is continuing till today. It would not be an exaggeration to say that, he was the greatest social reformer of his time. Because of this, wherever he went, his devotees started carrying out corresponding social reformist programmes. Nationalist leader Bal Gangadhar Tilak and other dignitaries were regularly visiting him for guidance and solace.

Shri Sai left his earthly body on 15th October 1918. His body was buried in the "Samadhi Mandir". Samadhi Mandir, Dwarakamayi Masjid, Chavadi, Lendi Bag, Gurusthan which is famous for the Neem tree with sweet juice and places like Khandoba, Hanuman, Ganesh and Shani temple are recognised as the favorite places of his devotees.

Sai Baba was not in favour of building any temples or institutions during his life time. The Shiridi Sai Baba Sansthan Trust is formed after his demise only and this trust is managed by the devotees. Now the Sai temple is controlled by a trust under the Govt. of Maharashtra. At present, Sai temples are established in every corner of the world. The founder of all these temples is Shri Chandra Bhanu Satpathy. Apart from it, hundreds of Sai literature and magazines are published in Indian Languages. The number of Sai devotees are also increasing unexpectedly.

There is ample communications to Shiridi from all over India. There are various hotels, devotees staying place (Bhakta Nivas), religious guest houses (Dharma Shala) etc. available for accommodation in Shiridi. Before leaving the body, Baba assured that his grave will talk. Among all the books written on Baba the "Shri Sai Satcharitra" written by Hemad pant is the best. Baba himself bestowed his Blessings for the writing of this book. This book is available in different Languages. All Sai devotees should read this book.

Four mass prayers are offered at Sai's grave (Samadhi-Sthala) every day. These aratis are performed at 5:30 in the morning, 12 noon, 6 pm at sunset and 9.30 at night. Apart from this, Satya Narayan puja of Baba is also held. Rama Navami, Guru Purnima, Dussehra days are celebrated with much pomp and ceremony. An average of 4-5 lakhs devotees visits Shirdi on these days. Palinki festival and procession (Patuar) are organised every Thursday. Now it is seen that the number of devotees in Shiridi is gradually increasing day by day.

The book "Shri Sai Satcharitra" is very useful. While reading "Baba's Leaving of body", Guruji totally lost his sense of time. Baba was suffering from slight fever on 28th September 1918. The fever continued for two to three days, but later, Baba gave up the food. As a result, he became weak gradually. After Seventeen days, on 15th October 1918 at 2:30 pm, Baba left his mortal body. (Shri Sai Satcharitra - 42 Part)

"His death is subject to an universal Law. He exists in all animate and inanimate objects and is the consciousness and enlightenment of all the elements. Those who worship Him with complete surrendering at his feet are still having and will continue to have such divine experiences". (Sai Satcharitra - 43-44 Part)

Baba's reassuring promise – "Even after passing in to Samadhi, I will continue to protect and guide my devotees."

He writes that Sai Satcharitra took him to Baba's kingdom and makes him very close to him. The biography of Sai Baba, his stories about animals and birds and his words are very amazing. It imparts wisdom and knowledge both on the worldly and spiritual level giving peace and contentment to the suffering human beings in this earthly world. The teachings of Sai Baba are very beautiful and instructive. All the desires of a devotee, who listen to it and meditate on it, are fulfilled like the bliss of meditation, mastering in eight-fold yoga and union with Brahma. (Shri Sai Satcharitra - Part 2)

Guruji Shri Satpathy continued to read Shri Sai Satcharitra for about three to four years. On the day of Mahashivaratri in 1993, he lit a lamp in front of the photo of Sai Baba, sat in one place and finished the reading (Parayan) of Shri Sai Satcharitra during that night. When he was going to Shiridi, he bought a bunch of Shri Sai Satcharitra books in English and Hindi and distributed them among the people. Sai Satcharitra is the medium which helps the devotees on their path of devotion. During Sai Baba's time, those who came in association with him have such important experiences. Some intellectuals like Dada Saheb Khaparde have recorded all this in their diaries. None of these are fictions. All those facts and characters are real. Baba had told clearly to Dabholkar, "I am writing my own biography". Hearing my stories and teachings will create faith and confidence in my ideology in devotee's hearts and they will easily get self-realisation and bliss. (Shri Sai Satcharitra – 2nd Part)

God is manifesting in every atom of the universe that surrounds humanity and living beings. A living being goes through the cycle of births until the result of his deeds (both good and bad) comes to an end. After the completion of Karma Phala (result of your deeds), there is no need to assume a human body. Then the soul no longer needs to take refuge in a body and it merges with the divine. The main duty of Shri Sai Nath was to rescue the human beings from the clutches of this dirty world and guide them to the path of liberation from the burden of their critical life. He has described many things about his past life in Shri Sai Satcharitra. Being the master of vast consciousness himself, he could know the state and level of consciousness of all souls and was also aware of their past births.

It should be the first and last aspiration on the part of a devotee to surrender completely before such an eligible Guru. Sadguru is the hope of liberation who is capable to guiding the human soul to its ultimate goal. Being above the cycle of birth and death himself, the Sadguru guides his disciples the path of their life, birth after birth. Father, mother and children are companions. But only the Sadguru is the companion after death. So all our faith, Love etc. should be placed at the feet of Sadguru with an unwavering faith and devotion one should realise that all the happiness and sorrows experienced in this life are at his behest.

Those whose faith and patience are stronger, the sooner they can realise themselves. For those whose faith is not complete and matured, the attainment is delayed and disturbed. Baba used to say that do not break down in any difficult situation, be patient, I will save you, this is my religion. Baba has given this assurance to all Sai devotees. What else com be expected more than this?

INFORMATION ABOUT OTHER SADGURUS

1) "Hazrat Babajan –

Her grave is now found under a neem tree in cantonment road, Pune. Hazrat Babajan is one of the India's most prominent female Sadguru. Such Sadguru is very rare in the world. It may be mentioned here that Hazrat Babajan's close relationship with Sai Baba may not be known to the Sai devotees

She was born in 1820 near Quetta in Beluchistan. She was named at birth as Gulrukh (face like a rose). After eighteen years, she left home to avoid marriage and fled to Rawalpindi and lived like a reclusive life for a few years. Probably she lived in a cave in isolation for seventeen months.

- Perhaps travelled to Punjab in 1845 and reached Bombay in 1900 and after some months went to east and north India.
- In April 1903, she went on a pilgrimage to Mecca.
- She again appeared in Pune between 1903 to 1907.

- Around 1920, she was established permanently under a neem tree in Barbabhadi, Pune. It was there that she assumed the name of Hazrat Baba. The meaning of Hazrat is presence and the meaning of Baba is father. She claimed herself as an older man. The meaning of Jan is life.
- She predicted a terrible storm around 1921. The common people of Pune built a house for her. The house was adjacent to the neem tree.
- Hazrat Babajan breathed her last in September 1921.

Hazrat Babajan was a saint who attained perfection like Shiridi Sai Baba. Most of the time she remained in meditation. Helping people became her daily routine. It is surprising to hear that she was able to lead a life as an ascetic despite being a woman. To know more, please read the book "Shiridi Sai Baba and other perfect masters" written by Shri Chandra Bhanu Satpathy.

2) **Sarmad – Iswar – Ek Madamuta**

Particulars of birth are not known. He was a Yehudi and came from Palestine. He was known as a business man. He was selling Persian blankets and dry fruits in India. This was during the time of Emperor Shahjahan (1628 to 1658). He came to Patna after receiving a divine call from Patna in Bihar. Then he left his profession to seek God and started settling in India. His fame grew day-by-day. Finally Emperor Shahjahan appointed him as the tutor of his son.

- Aurangzeb ascended the throne in 1658 and the Sarmad conspirators found a new lease of life. Sarmad was sentenced to death because he was walking around naked. But Aurangzeb was stunned by the divine events written by Sarmad. The punishment of death by beheading was given to him for declaring himself as "Mu Iswara (Amal Haz)".

- In the 17th Century, very few people in India and outside India knew about Sadguru Sarmad. Devotees still worship at his grave in Delhi (Near Jama Masjid). He came to India from Palestine during the period of Emperor Sahjahan. His main purpose at that time was to do various types of business. He used to bring dry fruits and blankets and take gold, silver, clothes etc. from India. He himself could not understand that when the creator had drawn him to Himself.

- Once while wandering, he saw a very handsome young man in Patna, Bihar. After seeing, a surprising feeling arose in his mind. "The Lord who has created such a beautiful human being, how beautiful He must be". Then "how to see God face to face" – this became his main task. He travelled repeatedly to different places such as big cities, forests, jungles, villages etc. to find God. Apart from it, he continued reading all religious books (Hindu, Muslim and other Scriptures). Because of this attitude, his friends who were very close to him, called him Mad. But he endured all the insults.

- In this state of mind, he went out to different places in search of any famous Saint to guide him. He met an ascetic Sadguru Vika who asked him to find the existence of God within himself. Almost all sages and great men give such type of advice. By Sadguru Vika's grace, a gradual mental transformation took place in Sarmad and he became fit to take the place of a Sadguru.

- Sadguru Sarmad always refused to do religious deeds like Kabir. But the followers of Aurangzeb did not like Sarmad much. They desired his destruction. At one point of time, while naked, Sarmad claimed himself as God and this matter was immediately reported to Aurangzeb by his faithful Maulabis and Qazis. Aurangzeb ordered his beheading as per Islamic Law. Sadguru Samad obeyed this order happily and smilingly. There was no disappointment of any kind in his mind. Rather he said "O God! You have come to me today in this condition." After his head was cut off, he stood upright and slowly walked up the steps of the mosque, holding the severed head in one hand. He wanted for God's justice. But his Sadguru told him not to do so, as it would surely have put Aurangzeb to death. He was such a Sadguru who finally invited death.

3) Shri Akkalkot Maharaj (An incarnation of Dattatreya)

Shri Akkalkot Maharaj is called as an incarnation of Dattatreya. Shri Dattatreya Abadhut is known as "Swami Samarth". Everybody in Maharashtra named him as "Swami Samarth". Nobody knows the birth history of Swami Samarth. He went on pilgrimage to various holy places like Puri Jagannath, Varanasi, Pandar Pur, Nishimawadi, Mangalawedha etc.

- He was seen in Akkalkot for the first time on a Wednesday in the month of Aswin in the year 1856 (September - October). He lived there for about twenty two years.

- Swamy reached Mangalawedha in 1838 and spent there for twelve years.

- He departed from Mangalwedha in 1850 and stayed in a place called Mohal for around five years. Later he went to some other places and reached Solapur.

- Swamiji arrived at Akkalkot in 1856 CE and resided in Khandoba temple. He took his meal at the house of Cholapa.

- In 1857, Kodak Photographic Company Photographed Swamiji for the first time. The presence of divine light was seen in that photo.

- He has shown many miracles during 1857-1858. Apart from this, he was the spiritual guide and religious teacher of many disciples. His disciples were Sri Badakar Maharaj, Sri Narasimha Saraswati, Sri Sitharam Maharaj, Jaban Aaalia, Sri Anandnath Maharaj, Sri Balapa Maharaj and others.

- In the month of Chaitra (April / May) in 1878, he merged with the banyan tree (Mula Purus).

There was very little difference between Swami Samarth and Shiridi Sai Baba. In the last moment of Samarth, he told his disciples that he and Sai Baba of Shiridi were one and same. He himself said that now he is residing in Shirdi and has moved from Akkalkot to Shiridi. A devotee Krishna Alibagkar started worshiping the Padukas of Swamy Samarth. In a dream at night, Swami Samarth appeared before Bagkar and said "I am now living in Shiridi, go there and worship me". Bagkar went to Shiridi and stayed there for six months. Later Baba said that what else is there in Akkalkot ? Now the Akkalkot Maharaj is residing in Shiridi. Then Bagkar realised that there is no difference between Swami Samarth and Sai Baba.

4) Shri Gajanan Abdhoot (Gajanan Maharaj)

- Nothing is known about his birth history.
- First appeared in Shegaon on 23rd February 1878. There, he was seen collecting ort foods from a dirt pile.
- He went to the house of Benkat Lal and stayed there. From there, he started his miracle activities.
- At morning 8 o'clock on the 8th September 1910, he breathed his last. Before taking his Samadhi, he had finished his worship to God.

There are no reliable facts about the birth history of Gajanan Maharaj. There is no proof, no writings available on his place of birth, date of birth and parents. Some say that he was born in Sajangarh, Maharashtra. It seems that the writings about the birth history of almost all saints are very little or not at all. They also do not tell anything regarding their birth particulars.

In the village of Shegaon in Maharashtra, a gentleman named Benkat Lal Agarwal first saw Shri Gajanan Maharaj while he was collecting residue foods from a garbage dump. On 23rd February 1878, Benkatlal had arranged good meals for the Maharaj. But Shri Gajanan Maharaj mixed all that food with the food he had gathered from the garbage dump and began to eat. Gajanan Maharaj was drinking water from the pond when Benkatlal returned from fetching good drinking water. Seeing all this, Benkatlal was fully convinced that he was a great man (Maha Manab). He bowed his head at his feet and begged his blessings. But by the time he raised his head, he had disappeared. Disappearance and reappearance is one of the eight Siddis.

It is seen in almost all Saints. Sadgurus and Qutbs reach their disciples at the right time, in this way, increasing the spiritual sense of the disciples.

Their actions are so intense that no devotee can resist it. Usually these Yogis do not want to live in anyone's house. They are not interested in caste, religion, sexual orientation, nationality etc. when Gajanan Maharaj stayed at the house of Benkat Lal, at his request, then, within a few days, thousands of people started coming to visit Gajanan Maharaj.

Shri Gajanan Maharaj was disappearing from time to time. May be that disappearance was to save a devotee. He might have gone to alleviate the suffering of a devotee. Hence saved a devotee from being stung by bees. But he took all those bites on his own body. He took a deep breath to avoid the mental agony of the devotees and immediately the bee stings fell from his body. To know more on the divine activities (Leelas) of the Gajanan Maharaj, please read the book "Shiridi Sai Baba and other Sadgurus" written by Guruji Satpathy.

5) Hazrat Baba Tajuddin

- Date of birth – 27th January 1861
- Place of birth – Kamthi, Nagpur
- His father died after one year of his birth.
- He received the blessings of Hazrat Abdullah Shah at the age of six. He said that Muhammad, the Abatar Purush, had descended on earth in the form of this boy.
- His mother expired when he was Nine years old.
- At the age of twenty, he joined the 13th Nagpur Regiment.

- In 1884, he met the famous saint Hazrat Daud Saha, after which he began to meditate and practice religious methods.
- After starting this, he resigned from the military service.
- On 26th August 1892, he was admitted in an insane asylum.
- In 1908, Maharaja Raghoji Rao removed him from the asylum and took him to his palace. Thus ended his sixteen years stay in the lunatic asylum.
- During 1920 to 1925, Baba's fame spread far and wide. He became known as the greatest Sufi Saint in the modern history. It is proved that his amazing achievements are of a very high standard.
- His soul merged with the eternal great consciousness on 17th August 1925.

At that time Hazrat Baba Tajuddin was one of the foremost Sadgurus. But this Sadguru was declared insane and was kept in the Nagpur asylum for over sixteen years. Baba, however, converted the asylum into a house of prayer. He did not cry when he was born. His father and mother tried hard to make him cry but to no avail. Finally the child cried as the hot iron struck on his forehead and ears.

To know more about Baba Tajuddin, Please go through the book "Shiridi Sai Baba and other Sadgurus" authored by Guruji.

6) **Sai Upasani Maharaj – A great creation of Shri Sainath**

- 15th May 1870 – The birth of Kashinath Gobinda Upasani Shastri

- 1877 – Sacred thread ceremony and formal anointing.
- 1884 – Ran away from home for the first time.
- 1885 – Death of the first wife and second marriage.
- 1886 – Ran away from home for the second time and then ran away again and again.
- 1890 – Visit Kalyan and be seen in a state of trance in the Vorgarh cave.
- 10th April 1890 – Pilgrimage to Omkareshwar, suffering from bronchial asthma and cured from it miraculously.
- 21st July 1890 – Returned to Satna.
- 8th August 1890 – Father expired on the day of Gokulastami.
- 1892-1895 – Studied Ayurveda and Sanskrit and started Ayurveda business.
- 1896 - 1905 – He did medicine business in Amaravati and Nagpur.
- April 1911 – Going in search of a Yogi for treatment of his respiratory problem.
- 27th June 1911 – First arrival at Shiridi.
- 6th February 1912 – He composed arati on Sai Baba.
- 10th August 1912 – Sai Paduka was installed under the neem tree.
- 18th July 1913 – As per the order of Sai Baba, Baba was worshiped as a guru for the first time.
- 1914 to 1917 – Upasani Maharaj travelled to Sikri, Nagpur, Shiridi and Pune. Finally settled permanently at Sikri.

- 12th December 1941 – He went to his birth place Satna for the last time and installed twelve Jyotirlings by his hand.
- December 1941 – He took his Maha Samadhi at Sakuri.

The full name of Upasani Maharaj was Sri Kashinath Gobinda Upasani Shastri. Later he was known as "Shri Upasani Maharaj." The most amazing thing was how this humble person could reach the Sadguru level in just four years. It was through Sai Baba's strange and difficult methods that propelled him to the rank of Sadguru. As a child, he was forced to drop out of the school due to the inhuman treatment of his teacher. Many people have seen him doing pranayama and various asans and chanting hymns. Finally he went to Shiridi and came in contact with Sai Baba. As a result, he was considered as one of the great Sages on the earth.

Upasani Maharaj was born on 5th May 1870 in Satna (Maharashtra). As a child, he was known as a very intelligent boy. At that time education was used only for livelihood purpose. So he gave up his reading in the middle. At that time, it was a common thing in the schools to hit the students by the teacher's cane. So he discontinued his study and left home after three years.

SHRI SAI QUESTIONS AND SOLUTIONS

On November 2002, Guruji Shri Chandra Bhanu Satpathy was requested to inaugurate the temple of Sai Baba in Chicago USA. More than 2000 devotees attended this Sai function. All these devotees were residents of United States of America, Canada, and Latin America and people from different religious families. This event lasted for three days. Due to infinite mercy of Baba, he spoke about Baba's life history and achievements. This was Sai Baba's first World Court (Darabar) where Sai consciousness and related facts were specially discussed. Similar world Court (Darabar) events relating to Sai Baba were also held in Australia, Johannesburg in Africa and Nairobi. After all these events, countless people from all over the world asked various questions through the website. Shri Satpathy decided to give answers to all these questions to the inquisitive and religious people. He tried his best to make the answers to the questions satisfactory. He decided to publish the questions and answers in a book form which was published as "Shri Sai Jingyasa O Mimansa".

Guruji's messages published in various Sai magazines during 2004 to 2009 have also been placed in this book. I and my intimate friends feel that this question answer book will provide various useful information to Sai devotees.

Now more than a thousand Sai temples have been built and many are under construction. Apart from this, worship and arati of Sai Baba is also going on in every house. Some devotees are worshiping the idol of Sai Baba by covering it with a piece of cloth and offering flowers and sandalwood paste. I know many working people keep an idol at their homes and pay obeisance before going to their offices or work places. It is their belief that if one goes out, after viewing (darsan) or prostrating before Baba, then Baba will protect him from any impending calamity. It is observed by almost all Sai devotees. Guruji has answered many questions on the website. All the answers are printed in a book "Shri Sai Jingyasa O Mimansa". It will not be easy to give all the questions and answers in this short book. Therefore, ten selected questions and answers are given in this book. If any Sai devotee wants to know more, then he can use the complete book "Shri Sai Jingyasa and Mimansa."

Q. No.1 – What does the word "Sai" mean? Who is Shiridi Sai Baba?

ANS. – The word Sai means – Saviour, Lord or God, Sadguru, ruler, king, Powerful person, father and even at times lover is addressed as Sai. Nothing is known till now about the name given to Sai Baba by his father and also his childhood. He is addressed by different names like Sai Ram, Shiridi Sai Baba, Sainath Maharaj etc. There is no doubt that he is above the spiritual achievements and an ascetic of self-realisation and sadguru class. He had spent almost forty years in Shiridi and passed in to Mahasamadhi on 15th October 1918. All his social, religious, spiritual and philanthropic activities were centered in Shiridi. Perhaps, for this, he was famous as "Shiridi Sai Baba".

Q. No.2 – Was Shiridi Sai Baba an incarnation or just a Sadguru?

ANS. – Incarnation is the birth of God Himself on this earth for the welfare of mankind. The work of Sadguru is to guide the devotees on the path of God and destroy the darkness by showing them the light of wisdom. But Shiridi Sai Baba is an incarnation of God (Avatar Purush) who took birth on this planet for the welfare of the human race. He lived like a poor Fakir. However, while immersed in spiritual frenzy, he is heard to have said before the devotees that "I am the God". Sai Baba was omniscient, omini present and omnipotent. He had complete control over the "Pancha tatwa" i.e. five elements (Earth, Water, Fire, Air and Space). These are mentioned in Sai Satcharitra. Sai Baba's Spiritual Power through out the world is evident due to the vast spread of Sai consciousness.

Q. No.3 – Heaven exists under the feet of Guru – How can it be perceived ?

ANS. – Service of the Guru's feet (Guru pada seva) is one of the Navadha (Nine ways of devotion i.e. Shravan, Kirtan, Smaran, Pada seven, Archan, Vandana, Dasya, Sakhya and Atma Nivedan) devotions prescribed in Hinduism.

After Guru leaves his mortal body, the pair of his feet should be the first concentration of the disciples. But the devotees of Baba have to meditate from feet to head and head to feet. Meditating on the Gurupada with concentration destroys all egos and creates a sense of total surrender within. While meditating on the feet, the disciple thinks of himself as a servant, not his friend. Sadguru is the source of all spiritual energies. We can possess spiritual powers by worshiping his feet, touching his feet, obeying his commands without any doubt and without any questions in our mind. Baba is not in his physical body now, but he will definitely help the spiritual upliftment of all the disciples. Guruji's own experience proves this. According to Guruji, Baba is the best Sadguru of this age. There is no doubt that Baba will help all his devotees even from his grave.

Q. No.4 – In which direction Baba's idol should be placed?

ANS. – The idol of Baba can be installed facing any direction. He was sitting in Dwarakamayi mosque facing west. In the burial temple (Samadhi Mandir), his head is towards north. However, his idol, which has been established here, is facing east. So it is better if the idol of Sai Baba faces east, north or north east. One more thing to be mentioned here is that any food cooked at home should be offered to Baba first and then distributed to the household members. For the worship of Baba, emotions are important, not the materials.

Q. No.5 – We have been committing many sins, both knowingly and unknowingly. Cannot it be prevented?

ANS. – Committing a sin knowingly and committing a sin in ignorance are two different things. It is more reprehensive and serious to do misdeeds while being fully aware. It is not so much a cognizable crime to have an insect trampled under our feet while walking on the road or by chance bumping into someone while driving. But if we do it knowingly, them it will be considered as a sin. There are two kind of sin i.e. Physical and mental. It is also a sin to harbour feelings of anger, violence and hatred towards others. Very few people think about the consequences of their actions. The work they are doing now may be good but it may be considered bad in the future. We should pray Baba to give us the power to distinguish between good deeds and bad deeds, give us the ability to judge the truth, guide us from the dark path to the light. These are what we should pray to Baba. If you read the life history of Saints and great men, you can know that how many difficult paths they had to pass to realise the God.

Q. No.6 – What is the role of temple patrons for pilgrims visiting Sai temples?

ANS. – The patrons must take care of all the requirements and necessities of the devotees visiting the temple. They should be alert to observe that the devotees become satisfied by having darshan of Baba. Proper maintenance of the temple after its establishment is of utmost importance. It requires planned effort. It would be better, if the patrons work in this direction in single mindset. The temple is built for the devotees. Therefore, it is necessary to show them gentle behaviour and listen to their grievances in an impartial and sensitive manner. It is not acceptable to give priority to one's family members or relatives in the temple.

Q. No.7 –   All my Life, I have tried to make others happy. But all I got in return was misery. Why did this happen ?

ANS. –   By doing benevolent deeds to others, you are expunging your sins. Your patience and forgiving qualities will make you Baba's favorite and all your good deeds are saved for the future. Be sure of it. But do not expect anything from a man. You will suffer a lot due to this. If you desire something then look towards Baba. You will be blessed in due time and your wishes will be fulfilled. Never deviate from your character. Pray to Baba to guide you always in the righteous path.

Q. No.8 –   What can a Sadguru do for a devotee? Why does he do?

ANS. –   Saints and Sadgurus are existing in both earthly and transcendental stages. They have passed through many births. In previous births, they have to suffer a lot like normal human beings. Through hard work, perseverance and penance they rise to the highest level. But they do not give advice to any one voluntarily (i.e. without being asked). Those who follow their advices are surely benefited. They protect the men from worldly pains and sorrows. They continue to resolve to guide them the way to liberation. They select one of the devotees as the future guru to carry forward their work in the next generation and groom him accordingly.

Q. No.9 – I want to know if the desire for sexual intercourse is an obstruction for attaining God ?

ANS. – For living beings, sexual pleasure is extremely satisfying and energizing. Sexual activity is the source of the growth of creation. The spreading in a species can be possible through the intercourse between a male and female. All religions and societies in all ages have accepted this Law of nature. This is inevitable. However, excessive sexual activity just for pleasure is harmful to the body, mind and soul. A lot of time is wasted in the desire of sexual happiness and its fulfillment. The meditation is interrupted. It is not possible to meditate on God or Sadguru with concentraton.. Therefore, do not succumb to intense sexual desire. Pray to Baba to give strength to the mind for this. Once in the Dwarakamayi mosque, Nana Chandorkar, who was sitting near Baba, was looking at a beautiful Muslim woman temptingly. The woman was removing her veil over her face. Baba could know Nana's mind and said "Nana, you are so restless for no reason. Let the senses do their work. Do not get involved in it yourself. God has created this beautiful creation. We have to enjoy it. The mind will gradually become calm and steady. Why come through the back when the front door is open ? Keep your heart clean, there will be no problem. The eyes have done their work, why are you so shy and worried ?" (4th Part Shri Sai Satcharitra)

Q. No.10 – Is there a rebirth ? Did Baba believe in it ?

ANS –   Yes; there is transmigration. If you will read Shri Sai Satcharitra, you will know that in previous births Baba had relationship with humans as well as with other animals, such as frogs, lizards, goats and tigers. Due to the relationship in previous births, the contact between humans and animals in subsequent births take place. According to the deeds (karma) or "Runanubandha" of the previous births, a person experiences happiness or sorrow in this birth. Baba said that a woman named Mrs. Khaparde was his sister in a previous birth. If we think that one birth is the beginning and the ending, that there was no birth before it or there will be no birth after death, then a huge question will remain unanswered. That is – why the neutral and merciful God has created this strange world where there are people with different abilities staying in different situations and some are suffering a lot whereas some are living very happily. Karma makes all the differences in this creation and this is a prominent aspect of Hindu philosophy. Without that, the neutrality and mercifulness of God would not be understood.

A BUNCH OF MESSAGES

Guruji sends four messages in a year for publication in various magazines. Those are New Year message, Rama Navami message, Guru Purnima message and Dussehra message. These messages are printed in Sai magazines on the above functions. Out of these messages, only two messages are written in this book which are worthy of study, can facilitate and signify the enthusiasm of Sai devotees. Sai devotees should read the book "Shri Sai Jingyasa O Mimansa" or all the messages of Guru (Guru Barta) published in "Sai Bani" to know about other messages.

Dussehra Message – 2007

(Dress code and certain rules of conduct while going to the temple)

When I go to Shiridi Sai Baba's temple or the conference of Baba's devotees, I have been observing that some so-called devotees come there dressed in unusual clothes and behave abnormally. I find it very inappropriate. It is polluting the pure environment of the temple. Even a common man with common sense can understand this. This does not require any deep analysis.

Our clothes and behaviour are determined by the locations and occasions. Would it be proper to come to the office wearing a wedding dress? There is a guide-line of wearing different clothes on each occasion in our society. Sikhs, Christians, Muslims and Buddhists wear specific attires and follow prescribed rules within there respective places of worship, such as Gurudwaras, Churches, Mosques and Buddhist temples. While inside the temple, our focus should be on Baba alone. All the senses should be directed towards Baba, (i.e. the eyes should be fixed only on the idol or vigraha, the voice should sing the hymns, the ears should listen to the arati and devotional songs and the nose should smell the fragrance of incense and flowers). The premises of the temple should be such that one gets spiritual peace in the chanting of mantras and singing the names of God. Loud talking as if attracting attention of others, laughing, jostling for darsan inside the temple are not acceptable at all. The sorrowful faces, tear-stained eyes of the devotees who have come with heavy hearts due to the non-realisation of their earthly desires, makes the atmosphere of the temple boring and joyless. During the arati the mind of all the devotees should be focused in prayer. Baba accepts only the unmoved, continuous appeal of the devotees.

May be an unknown person wears detestable clothes and speaks in a loud voice, then the attention of the devotees automatically falls on him instead of the idol (vigraha). As a result, the purpose of going to the temple of that person is destroyed. Talking or listening to music in a mobile has become a common thing now a days. It is not acceptable to change the moods of others by taking photos even inside the temple. Once Das Ganu Maharaj, with his team, came to Baba to perform Sankirtan. They were all dressed in colourful and jari laced clothes. In Maharashtra and other areas, kirtankars and katha bachakas (story tellers) almost wore such clothes, there was nothing unusual about it. However, Baba asked Das Ganu to give up his shiny clothes and wear as far as possible simple and plain clothes. Baba was testing his sincerity in the simplicity of the devotee's display of worldly grandeur through expensive clothes and ornaments. Therefore, it is desirable for everyone to attend the events of Sai devotees in simple clothes.

I have also noticed that some devotees wear kafni, like Baba and tie a similar piece of cloth around their heads. At the same time, some others hold a stick in their hands like Baba. But imitation of dress, behaviour, shape are prohibited in "Guru Geeta".

Swami Vivekananda never wore clothes like those used by his Guru Shri Ramakrushna Paramahans. Out of ignorance, a devotee may be following Baba and covering his body in such clothes, thinking that he is feeling better. Some vested interested persons are cheating money from simple minded devotees by dressing up as Baba and chanting Baba's name. The temple management executives should be alert and careful not to allow such cheats, treacherous, dishonest people to enter the temple or temple premises.

SOME OF THE EXCELLENT BOOKS WRITTEN BY GURUJI SHRI CHANDRA BHANU SATPATHY

GOPYARU AGOPYA

This book was published on 20th May 2010. The book was inaugurated by Hon'ble Governor of Odisha Shri M.K. Bhandare at the conference hall of May Fair hotel. I and my family participated in this function. This book is not related to Sai Baba's Leela. But Guruji says that such a book could be released only due to His Blessings. The main source of this book is the evolution process. We all think that the sun is the only stationary object in the solar system but the scientists have proven that our solar system is also moving. The system also orbits in the void holding its own planets and satellites. These facts are scientifically valid because the scientists have discovered many facts while researching on constellation of stars. One of these facts is that there are many solar systems like our Solar System (sun, planets and satellites) which are in motion as per the Scientific Law. According to the scientists, the motion of each objects depends upon the attraction of the other. The motion of these objects is determined by a scientific theory. Matter and materiality are not always the same. It changes over the passage of time. A scientist wrote about the black hole that, the materiality of the object increased abnormally, so that it loses all its lights. The materiality of any black hole is actually increased by manifold. For example, the materiality of a train on earth is almost the same as the materiality of a pea nut in a black hole. That means the ratio is greater than one million. The gravity of the black hole is also unimaginable. Before transformed into a black hole, the materiality of a fiery sun was normal. Due to the reduction in its lifetime, it underwent a downward transformation in materiality and converted in to a black hole. Half of the age of our sun has already passed and half life is left. That means the Sun's rays are continuously decaying and its decay is half the age of the original source, which is lakhs of million years. By the time this age is reached, all the planets, satellites may have been absorbed into the dark hole of the Sun.

What is written in this book is difficult for common people to understand. Even some educated people may not be able to understand regarding cosmology or Brahmagyana though they have a strong desire to know it. They cannot understand, not because of the language of this book but because of different principles described on the book. A common man cannot understand the cosmology, Brahmagyan, the origin and evolution of the universe. But if one reads carefully and tries to understand the hidden secrets of the universe, he will surely succeed, there is no doubt about it.

We do not know something or do not have the interest to know. This is nothing but your own ignorance. From Guruji's point of view and as per the opinion of the Scientists, this universe is infinite, immeasurable and also has birth and death. There is an immeasurable span of time between the birth and death of an universe. On the origin of the world, Guruji said – it is impossible to know the origin or the end of the mighty Jyotirlinga. The Jyotirlinga continued to grow upward and the Adilinga erupted at the top. There were eight eruptions inside it and new things came out on it. Too much heat, too much vibration and too much sound can cause the top of the "Hiranya Anda" to explode. Brahma appeared on the Lotus flower with the power of creation. There was vibration of primordial metals due to the eruption within "Hiranya Anda" and the universe is created by Brahma in the void.

Planets, Satellites etc. were born due to the explosion in the molecules of the star. All the planets continue to revolve around the sun (that star) and all the satellites revolve around the planets. It is not possible to calculate how many Solar systems are there in the universe, but life was born in the planet earth, and later these creatures lived in the air, on land and in water. It is not known whether there is life in other planetary systems or not. The scientists have also been examining for the existence of life on some of the planets in our solar system. Many Solar systems are reportedly exist in different positions of the universe. By the grace of the Lord of this universe, only man with knowledge exists on this earth.

The modern science is helping man a lot to know about the planets and satellites. Various mechanical knowledge and environmental theories are encouraging the scientists to learn more about the origin of planets, satellites and to know whether or not they are habitable. Recently a research has been initiated to know, whether it is possible to settle on the surface of the Mars. Research is also going on to determine whether it is possible to settle on Mars. The scientists have not withdrawn themselves from their goals, although this research is very expensive.

Guruji has written many things about Astronomy in this book. They are –

1) Philosophy (Tattva sastra) – i.e. Sunya Brahma Tattva, Pralaya Tattva, Aditya tattva, Ganapati tattva, Kala tattva, Rudra tattva, Swara tattva, Maha tattva, Nada tattva, Rusi or Debata tattva, Soma tattva, Narayan tattva, Narada tattva, Abatar tattva and Guru tattva.

2) Apart from it, the creation of the universe – Biswa mahajangya, Milky way, Naba Strusti, Sapta Jagat, Akanda Mandalakar Rupa, Mahasakti, Barna mala, Science of Creation, Pratika Brahma, Purusakar and last Prayer.

All these are very advanced poetry and easily understandable. Every Sai devotee and willing people of different communities should read it little by little.

Finally he wrote the character of human race. Humans are the best among all animals. O' Lord of the universe ! Please save this proud man, eliminate the habit of killing other animals to eat its meat. O' God ! victory to you and may the human race and various other races not perish from this world.

He wrote in the prayer –

"Let not men perish for pride
O' Lord, give us shelter at your feet
O' Void man, oh' above void Brahma
World is only part of you, you are the Purna Brahma"

Shri Chandra Bhanu Satpathy had learnt a lot about the Sanskrit Language from his late father Shri Gokul Chandra Satpathy. He says that this education helped him to compose this book. Some of his odia writings have been published in various comic magazines but he never expected to write on Cosmology, Narayanism, gravity and evolution. That too in fourteen letter Verses. He wrote that Sai Baba was very helpful in composing the book. He was deeply aware of this. Without Blessings, the composition of this poetry book would probably not have been possible on his part. It might be difficult to write a book on all these complex theories like solar theory, Cosmological theory and spiritualism. He wrote that some principles, he himself did not understand. Even some of the principles (i.e. Narayan principle, gravity etc.) were very difficult to understand. Gradually those became also comprehensible.

He writes that he often stands in front of Sai Baba's idol and makes mental preparations. Standing in front of Sai Baba's tomb and his idol in Shirdi, he spontaneously bowed down to him and accepted him as his spiritual master. Sai Baba always preached respect, ethics and tolerance. He was advising the devotees to have complete faith in the Guru. Baba had not much wealth. Before leaving the world, he had only a few clothes, a rag (kaupuni), a begging bowl and a broken mosque with him. He had also no heirs. He had nothing like Ashram, Trust, Temple etc. It is undoubtly true that thousand of devotees flock to his mosque to prostrate before him and to visit his idol even though he has absolutely nothing with him. This is my view point and that of almost all the Sai devotees.

This book is written in Odia language by Guruji Shri Chandra Bhanu Satpathy. Undoubtedly Odia is a very rich Language and influenced by Sanskrit. There was a time when people speaking other languages used to propagate Odia as a corrupted language of Bengali. Not only that, they also hated the Odia Language and Odias. I remember that in 1954 four of us travelled from Cuttack to Calcutta. We had taken our meal at a hotel near Calcutta deck. After our meal, the service boy called the owner different items with prices in Bengali. The hotel owner was writing in Odia on a board, but was talking with the service boy in Bengli. The manager told us that four meals cost five rupees. I asked him that he is writing in odia but speaking in Bengali, it is surprising. He said that we have all come from Kendrapada. We have studied through Odia medium, write in Odia and talk in Odia at home. But here, if you do not talk in Bengali, you would not get customers. This was the situation in 1954. Once we three friends were talking in Odia while walking on the footpath of Strand road. Suddenly a gentleman in suit boots asked in English, "what language you guys were conversing." He was very surprised when one of us told him that we were speaking in Odia. He had an impression that the Odias only know how to work as cooks, domestic servants and gardens. It means that there was no importance of any such language called Odia. The reason for this was that our Odia people are ashamed to speak in Odia outside. About this language Guruji Satpathy said that Odia language is a very Sanskritic language. In this Language, he describes the religious, philosophical and spiritual mysteries of creation in such a vivid and meaningful manner that the readers will understand them easily. In my opinion no language is inferior. Whatever language is understood easily should be the language of admiration for all. Only fools compare one language with other languages. There will be conflict and unpleasantness between different Languages. All should give priority to other languages along with your own Language.

In this book, Guruji Satpathy has explained the following topics in detail.

1) Ananta Purusha, Hiranya Garva – The origin of universe Hirany Garva,

   Hiranya Garva Sukta, Hiranya Garva – The origin of the universe (Bhagabat 5-20-48)

   Hiranya Garva – The origin of universe (5-20-44-45)

   Hiranya Garva – The origin of universe (Satpath Brahma 6-1-3-10)

   "Rudraya Agnimurtey Namah" – It is Shiva Puja Padhati.

   Hiranya Garva – Sesanath (Seshati Sankarsati iti Seshah) The second idol of the God.

   (N.B.- Hiranyagarbha - Literary meaning "golden womb". As per Hindu mythology Lord Brahma is considered to be this "Hiranyagarbha" as he created the world)

2) Sunya Brahma tattva – Sadhana Marg-3-1-21, Page-20

   Sunya Brahma tattva – Sadhana Marg-3-1-57, Page-21

   Karana Salila – Karan Rupi Sarobar

   Sunya Brahma tattva – Gyan Marg – 3-2-70 Page-24

   Sunya Brahma tattva – Gyan Marg 3-2-84, Page-27

   (Barah Puran, Trishakti Mahatmadhaya)

3) Biswa Mahayagna – Baiswarana – 4.2-26, 32 – Page-29

   Biswa Mahayana – Biswa Yagna – 4.3.44 – Page-34

   (Srimad Bhagabatam)

4) Adi Tattva – Siba Shakti kala - Kalahin Shakti (5.2-45, Page-41)

   Adi Tattva – Sibashakti kala (5.2-46, Page 412)

   (Srimad Bhagabatam)

5) Milk way – Description of space - Raj Nirghant – 6.1-7, Page-42

   Milk way – Description of space - Excerpt from Rug bed,

   Mahabharat and Matsya Puran

   6.1-12 - P.43

6) Pralaya Tattva - Black hole (7.1 -10, Page- 47)

   (A principle of great growth)

   The meaning of the word "Brahma" is "Brunhati Bardhate iti Brahma".

   Pralaya Tattva – Black hole (7.1-10, page 48)

   (After the light rays, energies are exhausted, that star turns into a black hole. Nothing, not even a ray of light, can escape its gravity.)

   Pralaya Tattva – Pralaya Dhara (7.3-62, 63, 64)

   (The meaning of Pralaya is kalpanta. The meaning of Maha Pralaya Brahma Pralaya or Naimattik Pralaya. Brahma Pralaya is created by Brahma. After Brahma there is Bishnu Pralaya and lastly Shiva's Pralaya occurs.

   Pralaya Tattva – Pralaya Dhara (7.3-71-55)

   Here is an article written by one of my students Dr. Sachidananda Padhy. How God manages the environment of creation in the Cosmic Context is described in the eighth and ninth chapters of the Gita and it is presented here.

"The principle of time who can understand,
He can know Brahma's day and night.
A thousand and four jugas are his day,
A thousand and four jugas are again his night.

At the beginning of Brahma's day all beings become manifested. In the night at the time of Pralaya everything is Lost.

In this way all the spirits, nature are repeatedly absorbed in the night and arise again in the day.

At the end of the cycle, all these beings merge into my nature. I create the living world once again at the beginning of the kalpa. The nature is created again and again by my influence. All the beings are under nature. They are helpless in the rule of the nature.

"under my Leadership the nature is created,
All the wheels of the world are being rotated."

From this presentation, it is proved that it is only under the Leadership of God that the creation begins and ends over the time, and also development and evolution take place.

The first five elements of immanent nature namely earth, water, fire, air and sky - are collectively called the five elements (Pancha Mahabhut)

The five elements of the ancient Indians were all basic elements and established as a inert factor (Manu 1/6, 20). The remaining three parts of the transcendental nature are mind, intellect and ego. All three behave in a passive manner due to the lack of conscious energy. The combination of mind, intellect and ego is called consciousness (chitabruti). At the beginning of the creation, nature grew and unfolded under the influence of cosmic intelligence, which is responsible for creation's ultimate destiny. Actually the limitless mature is the material world and the living world is pervaded by the connection of these two (Para and Apara)

7) Sutradhar (8-1, Page-58) Bishnu Puran 6-5

   Naba Srusti – Shweta Baman (9-1-19-20, Page-61)

   Tomo guna (ignorance, inertia, laziness) takes the form of Sattva Guna (Goodness, Calmness, Harmony) in the innovation & creation process.

8) Aditya Tattva – Rabi Narayan (11.1-1, Page-65)

   Bajamaneya Sanhita – 12-61

   Aditya Tattva – Rabi Narayan (11.1-3, Page-65)

   Haribansa 4-2 (Mundakopanisad 2-1-5)

   Verses on Sun – There are very bright stars in the sky. Science also proves the presence of many visible constellations in the sky like the sun. (Kriya Sara and Go rakhya samhita)

9) Ganapati Tattva – Description of Rudra (12-2-26 Page-70)

   Ganapati Tattva - Shiva, Parbati, Ganesh (12.3.58, Page-73)

10) Kala Tattva – Brahma kala and other kala (13.1.4.5. Page-75)

    The other name of nature – Sakti, Shangathar Padhati - Purba khanda 5th Part

    Kala Tattva - Brahma kala and other kala (913.1.18, Page-77)

The Sixteenth kala of Lunar cycle (Skanda puran)

Kala Tattva – Brahma Kala and other kala – Samani, Anjani, adikala - Bheda imaginary (kalpanik)

11) Rudra tattva – Subjugation of Rudra (14.1.5, 6, Page-82)

Seven States of fire

Bhed (excerpt from Haribansa Puran – Sabda kalpadrumre

Rudra Tattva – Agni Tattva – (Page-83): The intention of Goddess Laxmi was Amrit Janayatri Somashakti.

Rudra Tattva – Agni Tattva Page-84

Rudra Tattva – Para – Apara Power (Page-85)

Para Apara are the accumulation of eight parts of nature. Those are earth, water, fire, air and sky. Other three are mind, intellect and ego. The mind becomes more powerful of knowledge by the connection of consciousness of these three i.e. mind, intellect and ego. Indeed, the vast nature is the material world. The creation and expansion of the living world is pervaded by the connection of Para and Apara nature. From the scientific point of view, the cosmic force is – its own system of accepting the environment. Under the influence of this energy, the senses developed, so that the creature was able to perceive sound, touch, form, juice and smell.

Rudra Tattva – Uma and Shiva (A) The meaning of Uma is Amrit and Janayitri is Soma Shakti. (B) At the time of intense pralaya, Rudra incinerates everyone including the power of Uma. As a result, when the power is removed, the shakti in the form of Kalika dances on the Shaba (dead body) i.e. the powerless Shiva. Saptarsi Mandal (A constellation of seven stars). The word Rusi is derived from Rusi dhatu.

I want to write that

"Isha Basyamidam Sarb Jat kinchit Jagatam

Jagat ten tyakten bhunjitha ma grudhah kasya sidha dhanam (Jajur beda)

That means – "Everything (inert or consciousness) in this creation is covered by the God. Only enjoy the things left by Him. Do not covet."

Here the karma of humans as given in the Gita has been properly studied and the Karma has been discussed and presented comprehensively.

1) Adhisthan – All works are done by the help of human body.

2) Karta – The body and personality are the same. Whether the karma can be done or not is related to the relationship of these two.

3) Prakar karan – Man needs two reasons to do something.

   (i) Internalisation (Antah karan) – Internalisation is the reformation of previous births.

   (i) Externalisation (Bahita karan) – Externalisation is the five wisdom and five senses of this birth.

4) Try to do the work – Every kind of work is worth the effort. Without the help of senses, no work can be succeeded despite many efforts.

5) Daiba – Some say Luck. It is also called coincidence or God's dispensation. Some are born in a poor family

and rise up in the Society by their own excellence and some are born in a rich family and live completely unworthy.

According to Dr. T.N. Khusu (environmentalist), the universe and all the creatures living in it are the gifts of the God and they are related to the nature. No animal is superior then another animal. One should never surrender the fate of the nature in the hands of man (with all his great powers). It is never appropriate for any species to encroach forcibly upon the personal rights and privileges of nature of another species. Therefore, any living being should give up extreme greed and enjoy the bounties of the nature.

Who will say that those who try to launch nuclear bombs to make themselves superior will not backfire on them? Once, Prof. Einstein was giving a Lecture to a large audience about some nuclear weapons. One of the listener asked, what the shape of world war-III would be? In response, Einstein replied that he could not say anything about the world war-III. But he can talk about the 4th world war. This war will be fought with sticks, brick bats and stones. Because by them the nuclear war would have been over and few, if any, people who have escaped the world war-III would have had no knowledge of any kind of modern weaponry. Therefore, let it be our duty to warn the human society from now on.

All should give attention to the under noted sloka.

"Astadash Puranesu Byasasya Bachanam Dwayam Paropakaray Punyaya papaya Par Pidanam."

That means, the entire Mahabharat is written on sin and virtue. Sin is to hurt others and virtue is to benefit others. We do many things under the pretext of doing virtuous deeds but do not know whether it comes within the purview of virtue.

For example, it is not within the ambit of virtue to give good food to a well-fed beggar or brahmin and to deny or neglect or throw out a hungry beggar or blind man. Surely it can be called as a sin. So, my request to all the Sai devotees is to pay a little attention to this matter. Guruji has also given some lines like this in Shri Gurubhagabat, the meaning of which are not different from the above verses. Modern Scientists have presented some matters on planets and satellites, which everyone should know.

NASA (USA) continues its efforts to realise human presence on Mars. Each space shuttle will take a long time (several months) to reach this red planet. For this reason, the research is continuing on the effect of the health of humans and other accompanying animals. Recent research in Houston (USA) has shown that, the amount of water in the human body is around 60%. When a person falls from the void to the ground all his fluids (including blood particles) are forced upwards. It goes into the chest and head. The blood pressure in the brain inside the skull gradually increases. The research on the effects of these processes is going on.

According to Mark E. Kelly, a retired NASA scientist (Kelly went on four space shuttle missions before his retirement), the human body is not born to live in space. In order to move in space, you have to keep you head down for some time. Then return to steady state. For surviving in the space, one has to do like this always. Of course, this is his own opinion. He further said that apart from these processes, there is also fear of the bones breaking in to pieces. Other factors include the eating and sleeping problems. The NASA scientists are working hard to better understand and solve these issues.

Apart from this, there are different health problems that the doctors have been trying to solve since fifty years. It has been seen that an astronaut's eyeball was damaged due to going in to space. The biggest problem was radiation. Although earth's protective atmosphere and magnetic field absorb the radiation, it is not easily acceptable that the radiation field above the atmosphere will not cause cancer to the astronauts. However, the hard work and studies of scientists have helped for the reduction of this dangerous cancer attack. The scientists at the Johnson Space Centre (NASA's human infinite space flight plan) hope to send humans to mars by 2030. In between, they believe that the scientists will be able to examine and solve all problems. It is estimated that it will take about 20 to 24 months to reach mars and study various aspects. No astronaut has ever stayed outside the earth for so long. The current longest space flight is 438 days, which was accomplished by the Russian astronaut Valery Polyakov abroad the Mir space station (1994-95). Dr. Michael A. Barrett (NASA Astronaut) and Dr. R.B. Thirsk (also an astronaut) both experienced a difference in eyesight due to space travel. The scientists had realised that there was some change in their vision. Medical tests revealed that their optic nerves had swollen and affected their retina, which was reflected in the ultrasound images. After this test, NASA is forcing all astronauts to have their eyes tested before their Journey, Earlier nobody cared about the effect on the eyes. Who will tell that it does not affect the health, even if there is not much problem in the vision?

The Washington astronomers recently reported that

a never before seen river of hydrogen is blowing in the void of the sky at a distance of 2.2 billion light years from the earth's surface. Earlier the flow of Hydrogen River was not detected by the Scientists. This hydrogen river is heading towards Galaxy N.G.C 6946. This action possibly helps to create our various spiral galaxies and constellations. Where does the fuel come from to create it? The answer of this is that the scientists have speculated that the presence of these rivers may have been used as fuels.

According to some Scientists, Liquid Hydrogen rivers are flowing through the inter-galaxies. Under its influence, the construction of constellations may have been done easily. But this theory has not been proven so far. The reason for this is probably due to the lack of proper evidence. A spiral galaxy (like our milky way) creates the new Stars through secular evolution process. There are many galaxies in the infinite void. The scientists think that the power to these galaxies is probably given by such hydrogen rivers.

The Scientists have speculated that there is water on mars. If there is evidence of water on this planet then it is sure that there is life. Scientists believe that there are sulfur and magnesium deposits near the Sushev crater in mars. If came in contact with water, they would, no doubt, have been transformed to a salty state. This opinion is shared by almost all space scientists, there is no second opinion on it. But the discovery of ipsum salt and magnesium sulfate on the surface of mars indicates that water was abundant on mars. Gypsum or plaster of paris is usually formed when water flows through stones. It seems that there were water streams or reservoirs on mars a long time ago.

The MRO (Mars Reconnaissance Orbiter) Launched by NASA has sent some photographs to NASA which shows that the temperature on mars in summer is as low as -20°C and it drops considerably in winter. In the summer season, many channels like poles are seen, which are not visible in the winter season. This type of pictures were taken by space shuttle orbiting mars. It seems that the temperature of mars is –20°C and it goes down up to –100°C. This variation and very cold environment proves that life may not exist on this planet. We hope that in the future, the scientists will reveal more about true cause and existence of life.

As Mars is the nearest planet to the earth, Likewise the moon is the nearest satellite to the earth. No one can say that the atmosphere of earth will not be destroyed in a nuclear war. Therefore, scientists have been researching various processes to establish a settlement on the surface of the moon. These are the research processes. 1) Was there any life in this satellite earlier ? 2) Is the lunar surface fit for human habitation? 3) Oxygen levels in the moon's atmosphere, 4) Were there any vegetation or creatures on the moon before? 5) What is the state of water on the surface of the moon? If there is water, then how much and in which state. The scientists are continuing their research on these matters. Now it is known that, the moon is rich in magnesium, aluminum, silicon, potassium, thorium and uranium. All these metals can be used in various industries. But here I want to ask one thing that how all these metals or metal salts will be brought to the earth? The cost of transportation must be lakhs of times greater than the extraction cost from the mines of the earth. If the factory is established on the surface of the moon, then the cost will be unlimited, which is definitely not possible.

It should be noted here that radio-active elements do

not stay in one place. Its migration is according to the movement of air or water. In the Second World War, America dropped atomic Bombs on Hiroshima and Nagasaki in Japan. The second world war ended, within a few days of dropping of the bombs. Several days after the bombing, all scientists were stunned by a shocking incident.

The Siberian region remains frozen for most of the year. Here the Lichens are buried in the snow for several days. The name of this Lichen is Chadonia and this chadonia is the main food of the Balga deer. Another feature in this herb is that any poisonous liquid or vapour, in contact with it, once enters its body cannot come out again. This is because it has no Stomata in its body and what enters into the body will remain inside.

The examination of the dead Balga dear showed that the radio-active materials were abundantly present in the body. Exposure to this radio-active material is the cause of death of the Balga deer. Eskimos also get sick and die by eating the meat of this deer. All these events prove that the effects of radiation are not confined to one place. Radiation travels from one place to another with the movement of air or water and affects the living world. It we think that nuclear bombs exploded thousands of miles away will have no effect on us – This is not acceptable. There is no doubt that humans will be harmed by the nuclear bombs or other nuclear fallouts. It will affect all parts of the world and will undoubtedly cause the cessation of life.

Recently a group of researchers in London has researched on mars and provided some useful information. The purpose of the research was how the water in Mars had disappeared. Previously Mars was a source of water which was full of oceans, rivers and they were filled with water which started disappearing over the time. Now the water reservoirs on mars are in a drying state.

The scientists continue to research and collected data on various aspects of how the red planet's water had vanished and the planet became desert forever. The scientists have not yet been able to determine, what situation would have existed after a large portion of water vapours escaped from mars to the void. The new research indicates that the existence of cracks on mars confirms this idea. All mar's orbiting vehicles inform waterless river bed basins and even waterless oceans. Not only this, the presence of liquid water there indicates that living organisms lived in these places. Due to the low gravity of Mars, the water there could not be retained in the planet and because there was no barrier to the movement of water masses towards space, the water went in to the void gradually. Research has shown that water in the form of extremely hard condition, still exists in the two poles of the planet.

Earth is such a planet where billions of living creatures live in the water, on the soil, under the soil and in the air. During the day, the sky appears in blue, but at night, this vision disappears. At night the sky is dark and devoid of any light, only a few stars, planets and the moon are visible at different times. In the day time the sky appears in blue colour because this part of the light is scattered. The excess scattering is due to the fact that blue has a shorter wave length than other colours. This may not be correct and is worth testing. A few questions automatically come to mind here. Can we see all the planets and satellites ? Is our body able to see? The answer is that our eye sight is not able to see objects that are far away with the naked ayes, but we can only see a small amount if these objects are scattering light. We are able to see them through binoculars. In the dark night, if any place is illuminated by light then we can see it with our physical eyes.

Almost all the planets and satellites of the universe are without any living beings. Earth is the only planet where different kinds of life exist. So far only planet earth is home to the living world. Here plants, animal world and different types of organisms such as bacteria, viruses and single-celled or multi-celled creatures live on land and in water. Up to now there is no evidence of the presence of life in any other planets or satellites.

According to a recently published report, various scientists have expressed their concern that large volcanoes on Mars may have caused problems for the survival of life there. Different experiments have yielded different results. Recent experiments show that large scale volcanoes once existed on this planet which is twice as tall as Mount Everest. The largest mountain in our Solar system, Arcia Mons, is situated on Mars and it contains the largest volcano. The animal world there would have been destroyed due to the volcanic eruption. Of course, it is not known, till now, whether the animal would exists there or not. All these facts are based on NASA's Mars mission data analysis.

"DO NOT FEAR DEATH" – AN IMPORTANT ADVICE FROM SAI BABA

A person who takes shelter in God becomes free from fear. Every moment should be rectified to reform the death. The desire is the result of your previous births. If concentration does not come while meditating then think of Sai Baba or any deity repeatedly. The final test in human life is death. He whose life is improved, his death is also simplified. The one whose time has improved knows the value of time. Therefore, every moment should be used appropriately.

Every Sai devotee should remember these advices. One more thing I would like to say to all the Sai devotees that they should ask themselves "who am I?" Is that the name given by father, mother or any elderly father-like person? If one calls in that name frequently, then everyone will start calling in that name only. I will also begin to associate that name with good or bad deeds. That I am unique is an illusion. The day will come when I will be sorry for my existence. Man is a representative of the living world and all the creatures living in this world are dependents of God. The creatures dependent on God should never be afraid of death.

Meditation on God is a spiritual practice that keeps

the meditator away from other wordily activities. Sometimes a person sitting on meditation is not aware of what is happening around him or he has lost his desire to know it. This process of meditation is time consuming and not everyone (who is bound to the family) can have time to meditate. Therefore, worship of Sai Baba is the only simple way by which spiritual work is accomplished automatically. In this chapter, the simple worship method of Sai Baba is described which is written by Guruji Shri Satpathy himself.

THE SIMPLE WORSHIP METHOD OF SAI BABA

Pujya Guruji Shri Chandra Bhanu Satpathy is often asked by the Sai devotees about the method of Baba's worship and special rituals. Some Sai devotees also ask a lot about the preparation of the prayer-place where they will worship Baba. Sometimes he would explain the answer very clearly and sometimes he would explain to him in detail how to do the worship. The questioner (Sai devotee) cannot remember everything and many devotees do not have access to Guruji easily. Probably, due to all these difficulties faced by the Sai devotees, he wrote the book on simple worship methods of Sai Baba which would be useful to all the Sai devotees.

Many a times we worship the gods without knowing the proper procedure. If we will do so, may be our inability to worship will be reflected in it and many questions arise in the mind. Am I doing it right? Is not it wrong to do so? The answers to all these questions have been briefly written by Guruji Satpathy in this book. In this book, the worship procedure for Sai Baba is described in a simple and easy manner. Sadguru Sai Baba has provided shelter to everyone in this world and is always trying to liberate them from this world. This Sadguru is the great mountain of forgiveness and peace who can liberate us from this ocean of worldly existence. There is no doubt that Baba's Blessings must save us from the ocean of worldly illusions, even if it is very deep.

1) SPECIAL WORSHIP:

The special worships of Baba in Shiridi take place on certain days. The devotees can also perform these special worships of Baba, as per the tradition of Shiridi on the following days at their home.

- Rama Navami (Birth day of Baba)
- Guru Purnima (worship of the Sadguru)
- Dusherra (Mahasamadhi day of Baba)

Apart from it, Krishna Janmastami and Mahashivaratri can also be celebrated. Puja should be done in "Panchopachar" method or if one is capable enough then in "Sodash Upachar" method.

(N.B. – In Panchopachar puja, offering to the God consist of five items representing the five elements of which the universe is comprised. They are Gandha (representing earth), Puspa (ether), Dhoopa (air), Deepa (fire) and Naivedya (water).

Sodash upachar Puja – (sixteen step puja) where each upachar is a service to the deity. They are Darsan, Aradhana, Asana, Paadya, Arghya, Achhaman, Snaana, Vastra, Yognopaveeta, Gandha, Pushpa, Dhoop, Deepa, Naivedya, Tambula and Pradakshina and Namaskar).

During the puja, arati should be performed with bhoga. Prasad can also be distributed to the poor and destitute persons apart from family members. If desired, donating food or Langar (mass feeding) can be provided through the local Sai temple.

THURSDAY PUJA

- Thursday is observed as a holy day every week due to the worship of Guru.

- On these days the devotees can recite the Sai Satcharitra at home privately and collectively in the temple and meditate on it as per the instructions written in the book.

2) DAILY WORSHIP

Devotees should accept the current worship practice of Sadguru Shri Sainath in a very simple and easy way. If we analyse only the feelings of the devotees of Shiridi during Baba's time, it is clear that the kind hearted Sai Baba wanted only easy and simple devotion from the devotees. A piece of bread donated by a poor devotee with utmost devotion gave him great satisfaction while the delicious food served on a silver plate by the rich man was generously shared among all. He was going to beg for alms from the houses of devotees. Baba happily accepted the simple foods like bread, bhakari, pulses, greens and curry received from every house.

3) RULES OF WORSHIP

- Daily worship of Baba does not require external pomp and expensive Puja items. Any member of the family such as father, mother or adult son, daughter can perform this puja.

- If the member who performs the prayer daily remains absent for any reason, then any member of the family can perform the same in his place.

- If the entire family goes out of the house for some work, them this work, can be done by any of their related Sai devotees.

- If there is capacity, an outside worshiper may be engaged to perform the Puja in the absence of the household members.

- If this is also not possible, then one should close and leave the house to anywhere only after worshiping Baba's idol and covering it with a red or yellow cloth. The worshiping can be started as usual, after returning home.

- If possible, when the whole family leaves the house, the head of the family or his wife should carry a small box with a small idol or photo of Baba and some necessary puja items and utensils. He can worship this idol or photo wherever he goes. This type of worship can be done anywhere in the country and abroad.

- It is good to take Shri Sai Satcharitra book with you for reading.

4) **PRASAD**

- Dry Prasads Like gram, almond or Peanuts, mishri, ukhuda, khai etc can be offered to Baba.

- If possible, daily home-cooked meals can be served at noon or night in a plate and/ or bowl specially meant for Baba. It is customary in Baba's time to mix the food offered to Baba back in to the food bowl and accept it as Prasad. Therefore, it is correct to do so.

- But it should be done according to the strength and ability of the devotee, not under compulsion or in imitation of someone else.

5) **PADUKA PUJA**

- As per the custom in Shiridi, the bathing water of Baba's idol can be accepted as Paduka water.

- The place where the sandals (Paduka) of Guru are placed can be washed and the water can also be used as Paduka (Prasad).

- Some devotees bathe Baba's idol or Paduka with Panchamruta. That panchamruta mixed with water can also be taken as Paduka.

6) **ARATI**

- Now-a-day's four main aratis are performed daily at Sai Baba's Samadhi mandir in Shiridi. They are (1) Kakad or morning arati (4.45 AM), (2) Madhyan or day time arati (12.00 noon), (3) Dhoop or evening arati (6.30 p.m.), Seja or night arati (10.30 p.m.). It may not be possible to perform all these aratis at the home of devotees.

- Therefore, the morning and/or night arati should be done collectively by the family members.

- If the arati is not remembered, then arati can be done by playing an arati CD.

- In this way, the arati will be memorised gradually.

- The meaning of these aratis written in Marathi Language should be understood. If you do arati without understanding the meaning, then the devotions, emotions may not be fully awakened within you.

7) **UDI OR VIBHUTI**

- Baba's Udi or Vibhuti (holy ash) is available in Shirdi

and the packets of Vibhuti are also sent by post by the Shiridi organisation to the devotees who have registered their names.

- It should be collected from the temple while travelling to Shiridi and kept at home.
- It should be taken with water after worshiping and before going to bed at night and can be applied on the forehead.
- The devotees can take this Vibhuti along with them to use while going out.
- While distributing Prasad at home, one should also distribute Vibhuti.

8) **THE CLOTHES OF BABA**

- Many devotees, at their home, bring clothes to be worn by the idols or Photos of Baba. The clothes of Baba are of special type. Usually Baba is dressed in under garment and a beautiful garment over it. A small piece of cloth (Patka) is put around the head.
- Keeping three or four pairs of yellow, orange, blue, red etc. clothes at home will be enough.
- A special pair of clothes can also be worn on special festival days such as Rama Navami, Guru Purnima, Vijaya Dashami and Thursdays.

9) **THE USE OF OTHER THINGS BY BABA**

- A crown made of metal or other materials is worn by Baba in the temple or in the house. It should be remembered that this crown should be removed before Seja arati.
- Many people also keep tweezers, hookahs and chillum

pipes near the statue or photo of Baba. It can be followed as it is the prevailing practice of Shiridi.

10) WORSHIP BY THE DEVOTEES IN THE TEMPLE

- The devotees of Shirdi Sai Baba visit the temple frequently, have a view (darsan) of worshiping procedures (Puja upachar) and often sing the arati in congregation. While staying in the temple, the following matters should be kept in mind.

- One should behave with peace and order within the temple premises and should not interrupt the worship, arati or meditation of other devotees by talking in loud voice.

- The time inside the temple should be spent in Baba's prayer, meditation and arati. It is not advisable to waste time and spoil the atmosphere by different types of family and social interactions.

- Often, one has to move in a queue when going for Babia's darsan. He should proceed orderly in that time. One should keep his small children under his control while inside the temple.

- Elderly men and women, disabled and sick devotees should be given priority to get Baba's darsan and they should be helped as much as possible for this.

- The rules of the temple should be followed strictly because during Baba's life time in Shiridi, the devotees used to move around in a disciplined manner as per the order of Baba. This practice is still prevalent in Shiridi.

- One should keep his mobile phone switched off during the puja and arati as it may disturb the worship and meditation of other devotees.

- In the Sai temples where there is facility of mass feeding, special worships, such programmes can be conducted as per the temple rules. It is not appropriate to break the rules in this regard.

- Every day prasad is offered to the deity in the temple. In violation of this rule, one should not accumulate home-made foods in the temple. Permission of the temple authorities should be obtained before conducting such a programme.

- If there is a desire to offer some items such as Baba's clothes or other items of worship to Baba, it should be given to the temple through the temple authorities.

- Any personal worship or personal works should not be performed by the priests of Baba's temple. All should co-operate to help the priests to fully engage in the worship of Baba.

- While in the temple premises, one should be vigilant to keep the temple neat and clean. The temple should not be defiled for any reason.

- Any problem or disturbances faced during prayer and arati in the temple should be resolved peacefully by discussing with the temple authorities.

- It should be remembered that worshiping with devotion to Baba in home, temple or elsewhere is the main purpose of the devotees and this should be their aim. We should not do any such work at home or in the temple which will distract us from our aim. It is clearly mentioned in Shri Sai Satcharitra that only the calm, pure and devoted people become Baba's favorite and receive His divine grace.

- The palanquin festival of Baba is held in many temples on the above mentioned special days and on Thursdays. The devotees are very eager to carry Baba's palanquin. There is a chance of injury by pushing, tripping at the time of palanquin festival of Baba. The palanquin should be carried by keeping this situation in mind. If any devotee falls down and gets injured during this time, priority should be given for his treatment as soon as possible. It is the prime responsibility of every one to follow the rules imposed by the temple authorities while this programme is going on.

- Sometimes, on temple foundation day or other special days, special cultural programmes are organised which include playing of devotional music, children's dance programmes and dramas based on Baba's life history. It creates a spiritual atmosphere and sense of unity among the devotees. This programme should be enjoyed with respect and devotion.

- It is not desirable to display one's wealth, name, fame or power in direct or indirect manner while in the temple premises. Baba used strict rules to keep such people under control in Shiridi.

SHRI SAI MANTRA WITH MEANING

"Hiranyagarbhasambhutam Sriman Narayan Sai". This mantra should be used individually or collectively as an invocation mantra before morning worship at home, temple or any institution related to Baba. By listening this sai mantra CD or singing it, the experience of divine bliss awakens in the mind. By this mantra the Sadguru can be invoked in the form of any deity and get the fruits of worshiping that deity.

Hiranyagarbhasambhutam Sriman Narayan Sai.
Sachidananda Parambramha Sriman Sadguru Sai
Anistanashak Gyanadata Ganapati Shri Sai
Palanhari dayasagar Vishnurupa Shri Sai (1)

I take refuge in Sadguru Sainath as Satchidananda Parambrahma who appeared as Narayan from Hiranyagarbh. He is the symbol of Ganapati (Ganesh) as destroyer of all harms and obstacles and the giver of wisdom and also all pervasive power of Vishnu as the lord of sustainer of the creation.

Dwandwatita - Trigunarahit Sadashiv Shri Sai
Srusti niyanta chaturbed datta Brahmadev Shri Sai (2)

You are the supreme benefactor Lord Sadashiv and

the controller of the creation. You are Brahma, the manifester of four vedas, you are Dattatreya and Brahmadev yourself. I take refuge in you.

> Rudrabatar Bhakat Shiromani Paban Putra Shri Sai
> Tridebputra Abadhut Dattatreya Shri Sai (3)

O Sai, you are the incarnation of Shiva (Rudra) and the son of Pavan dev (God of air) as well as the foremost devotee of Shri Hanuman. O' Sainath, you are Abadhut Dattatreya, the embodiment of the combined powers of three gods i.e. Brahma, Vishnu and Maheswar. I take refuge in you.

> Brahmaswarupini Parabidya Gayatri Shri Sai
> Rakhyakarini Mahasaktimayee Mahadurga Shri Sai(4)

O' Sainath, you are the source of Chinmaya Shakti, the all-pervading consciousness of the supreme being. You are above the ved- vedenta, you are the Brahma Shakti Gayatri, the combination to all the virtues of Bhagawati, Mahalaxmi, Saraswati. You are the basic power of Maha Durga, the destroyer of all evils and the protector of virtuous beings. I take refuge in you.

> Astasidhhi Nabaratnadatri Mahalaxmi Shri Sai
> Kalaprabina Bidyadatri Saraswati Shri Sai (5)

O' Sainath, you are personified by the power of Mahalaxmi, the giver of eight Sidhis such as Anima, Laghima, Prapti, Prakamya, Mahima, Isitwa, Basitwa and Kamavasayitwa, and Nabanidhis such as Pearl, Manikya, Baiduriya, Onyx, Diamond, Coral, Padmarag, Emerald and Nilakanta Mani. Epitome of knowledge given the Saraswati Shakti, expert in sixty four talents such as song, music, drama, painting, poetry etc. I take refuge in you.

> Sakar rupa Nirakar Ananta Puran purus Shri Sai
> Swikar karo Pranam Mera Bhakta Bastsal Shri Sai (6)

O' Sainath, you are the great adi purush of veda, the shapeless void Brahma. O' Saviour of devotees, Sainath. I take refuge in you. You accept my obeisance.

(The devotees can learn the style of chanting of this mantra composed by Guruji Shri Chandra Bhanu Satpathy by listening the CD "Hiranyangarva Sriman Narayan Sai" prepared by the "Saregama" company.

"Shri Sainathay namo namah"

Remembering or reciting this great Gurumantra in the morning will make the devotee's heart steady and happy. While at home, outside home, moving in a vehicle or doing any other activities, chanting or listening to it at any time will bring peace and bliss to the mind. It can be used on special occasions, especially on auspicious days like Rama Navami, Guru divas, Mahasamadhi divas and Mahashivaratri.

> Shri Sainathay Namo Namah
> Shri Satchidananday Namo Namah
> Shri Mangalamurati Namo Namah
> Shri Gurucharanabhyam Namo Namah.

I bow to Shri Sainath. Obeisance to Shri Sainath, the root of truth, consciousness, bliss (sat, chit, anand). I prostrate before Sadguru Shri Sainath, who has incarnated for the welfare of the world. O' Sainath, I offer my obeisance at your feet.

> Shri Sainathasya Charanam Sada Smarami
> Shri Sainathasya Mahima Sada Bhajami
> Shri Sai Pujanam Nityam Karomi
> Shri Sainathaya Sharane Sada Gachhami

I will always meditate on Shri Sainath's foot prints in my mind. The singing of Shri Sainath's virtue is my best hymn. I will always worship Shri Sainath and take refuge in him.

> Jaya Jaya Mahantam
> Jaya Jaya Karunanidhanam
> Jaya Jaya Abadhutarupam
> Jaya Jaya Sai Mahantam
> Jaya Jaya Karunanidhanam

Victory be to the great guru shakti Shri Sainath. May the great grace power of Sainath be victorious. May the embodiment of greatest Saint Swami Shri Sainath be victorious.

> Mama Hrudayakunje Nibasam Kuruhe
> Sainath he Sadguru
> Shridebaputra he daibishakti
> Dehimamachala bhakti

O' Sadguru Sainath, may you live in my inner heart, O' son of Narayan, O manifest divine power, bestow unceasing devotion on me.

(The devotees can learn the style of chanting of this mantra composed by Guruji Shri Chandra Bhanu Satpathy by listening the CD "Shri Sainathay Namah Namah" prepared by the "Saregama" company.

"Tubhyam Namami"

This Sai mantra can be recited especially on important days like Thursday, Gurudivas, Ekadasi, Mahashivratri etc. and also with parayan. It can also be chanted after or before any arati in the temples. It is a description of the timeless and divine form of Sadguru Shri Sainath Maharaj. If you remember this in the core of your heart, it will be easy to connect with Sadguru.

> Tubhyam Namami Sainathay
> Tubhyam Namami Narayanay
> He dinabando tubhyam Namami
> Tubhyam Namami Jagadiswaray
> Tubhyam Namami Sainathay. (Ghosa)

Hail to you Sainath. Salutation to you, O Sai-Narayan. O friend of poor, O the God of universe, Salute to you again and again.

> Tubhyam Namami Sainathay
> Tubhyam Namami Madhusudanay
> He Bhakta pran Tubhyam Namami
> Tubhyam Namami Basudebay
> Tubhyam Namani Sainathay... (1)

Hail to you Sainath. Salutation to you, O' Sai – Madhusudan. Salutation to you, O' Sainath, Devotee's life line. Pranam to you, O' Sai – Vasudev Srikrishna.

> Tubhyam Namami Sainathay
> Tubhyam Namami Kalatitay
> He Muktidata Tubhyam Namami
> Tubhyam Namami Abadhutay
> Tubhyam Namami Sainathay. (2)

Satulation to you O' Sainath, Hail to you, O' infinite eternal Sadguru Sainath. Hail to you, O' liberating Sainath, salutation to you O' the great ascetic Sainath.

> Tubhyam Namami Sainathay
> Tubhyam Namami Anantay
> He Krupasindhu tubhyam namami
> Tubhyam namami Jogirajay
> Tubhyam Namani Sainathay (3)

Obeisance to you, O' Sainath
Salutation to you, O' eternal anecestor Sainath
Salutation to you, O' Sainath, the ocean of kindness
Tubhyam Namami Sainathay
Tubhyam Namami Satchidananday
He dayasindho tubhyam namami
Tubhyam Namami Jagannathay
Tubhyam Namami Sainathay ….. (4)
Hail to you, O' Sainath
Salutation to you, Sainath, the embodiment of truth, consciousness bliss.
Pranam to you, O' Sainathy, the ocean of mercy
Salutation to you, O' Sainath, the lord of the universe
Tubhyam namami Sainathay
Tubhyam namami Dattatreyay
He Kalpabrukhya tubhyam namami
Tubhyam namami Parameshwaray
Tubhyam namami Sainathay ……. (5)
Hail to you, O' Sainath
Salutation to you, O' Dattatreya Sainath
Salutation to you, O' Sainath, the Omnipotent tree (Kalpadrum, a tree that yields all one desires)
Hail to you, O' Sainath, the Supreme Land (Parameswar)
Tubhyam namami Sainathay
Tubhyam namanni Sidhhidatay
He shantakar tubhyam namami
He Guromurte tubhyam namami
Tubhyam namami Narayanay
Tubhyam namami Sainathay ….. (6)
Salutation to you O' Sainath

Hail to you, O' Sidhidata Sainath (Ganesh, the bestower of success and accomplishment)

Salutation to you, O' Shiva – Santakar - Sainath

Namaskar to you, O' Sainath, the source of divine power.

(The devotees can learn the style of chanting of this mantra composed by Guruji Shri Chandra Bhanu Satpathy, by listening the CD "Tubhyam Namami" prepared by the "Times Music" company.

SOME INFORMATION ABOUT A FEW SADGURUS AND SAINTS

I want to say here that, no matter who the Gurushrestha is, he does everything only for the betterment of the country. An instance of this is presented for the knowledge of the devotees. There are many examples of judgments in the history of India. Some Hindu kings do not hesitate to donate their kingdoms to others. Such an incident took place during the time of Maratha hero Shivaji. Ramdas, the guru of Shivaji, used to go from house to house for begging while saying "Jaya Raghuvir Samarth". As soon as they hear the sound of this word, the women pour rice from their houses, in the bag of the Guru. When the great Guru Ramdas went to Shivaji's palace, Shivaji donated the entire Maratha region instead of alms. Despite many denials and explanations by Gurubar, Shivaji did not agree and handed over the governance of the Maratha kingdom to the Gurubar. At last Gurubar asked Shivaji, what will he do with the kingdom? Shivaji told that "you can do whatever you want, because now the kingdom is yours and you are it's ruler." Then Gurubar said that if he is the king then Shivaji is his subject and the subject is bound to obey the king's order. His mandate was that Shivaji would administer the Government on behalf of Guruji and protect the country from the enemies. This order of Gurubar remained in force.

Saint Gyaneshwar

Hear I am trying to write something about saint Gyaneshwar. Even, now a days, in Maharashtra the book Gyaneshwari (a compilation of the Gita in Marathi with translation and commentary by saint Gyaneshwar) is still read in villages. Who is saint Gyaneshwar? I am writing below something regarding this matter.

In Alandi village in Maharashtra, Bithalpant left his wife Rukmini Bai and went to Banaras to become a monk without telling anything to anyone. He became a disciple of Swami Shri Ramanand at Banaras. After some time Guru Shri Ramanand Swamy had come to Alandi (village of Bithalpant) and there he met Rukmini. During the meeting, Guru Shri Swami blessed Rukmini Bai for a happy married life. While crying Rukmini Bai told Guru Shri Ramananda Swami that this blessing would never be possible, because her husband had left Alandi, and now a disciple of Shri Ramananda Swami in Banaras. When Shri Ramanand Swami came to know that Bithalpant was his disciple and married, he immediately left for Banaras. On reaching Banaras, he forced Bithalpant to return to Alandi and resume his married life. Under compulsion, Bithalpant reached his village and settled down with his wife. At that time, there was a rule that if a man became a hermit some time after his marriage and return home afterwards, then he had to live as a Chandal outside the village. As per this law, Bithalpant lived in a hut outside the village. The first child of his father, Nibrutinath was a disciple of Gahininath. The second son, Gyaneswar, was the disciple of his own brother. Afterwards, the spiritual knowledge of Gyaneshwar was greatly enhanced, so he became famous as saint Gyaneswar.

He had memorised the entire Vedas, and even many legends about his miraculous life are available in the State of Maharashtra. His sister Muktabai was a famous Yogini.

Brahmins usually hold various competitions to test their erudition. Once a competition was announced on the excellence of Veda reciting and Veda reading. Brahmins come from many places to participate in it. Saint Gyaneswar also reached the venue to take part in that competition. Ironically, he was abused and threatened to leave by the Brahmin community. Before leaving, Saint Gyaneswar said "the Vedas you are reciting is nothing – a buffalo can recite the Vedas too." When a buffalo was brought and placed in the contest place, Gyaneswar spoke something in buffalo's ear (probably a mantra), by which the buffalo started chanting the Vedas clearly. After that he left the place. The explanation of Bhagavat Gita is Gita Gyaneswar which is being read all over Maharashtra especially in villages. When Saint Gyaneswar realised that his work in this world was completed, he asked his disciples to dig a pit under a Neem tree. He sat in that pit and fixed his body by applying the final action method. This tomb is called "Jiba Samadhi". The grave was buried and a burial place was made. Even now people believe that Saint Gyaneswar exists there in a subtle form. He is known all over Maharashtra as a famous Yogi. "Gyaneswari" written by him, is more popular than the Gita in Maharashtra.

The different experiences in Shiridi by another Himalayan Yogi are given below. The Himalayan Yogi had not decided anything before going to Shirdi. But it was the order of Saint Gyaneswar that, he would go to Shiridi and have a view (darsan) of the "Asthan" of Sainath. At last it happened like this. The Yogi went to Shiridi and reached late at night. An anchorite (Babaji) was standing at the door of the tomb. That was night time and Chavadi was not open. Shaking the door revealed that it was locked from the inside. But the hermit (Babaji) told him to close his eyes and go inside through the door. When he got near the door, he felt something like a cloth (dhoti) was laying there. Pulling the cloth to one side, the two people went inside. The hermit said to open his eyes. The stranger perceived as if he had drawn back a curtain and entered inside. There were four lamps burning inside and a narrow wooden plank was hanging by threads, made of torn clothes, tied to it. Sainath was sleeping on it. He was astonished. Sai Baba passed away many days ago. Now how was he seen here? Apart from it, how would he get down from the seven feet high torn swing? It appears that he slowly get down from the swing like swimming in the air.

Sai Baba embraced the hermit in muslim tradition. Both of them kissed each other. The yogi was wonderstruck to see all this. He blessed the Yogi and said this Guru of yours is great, Allah Mallik, Rama Rama. He also asked the hermit to bless him. He blessed the young man and gave him a bundle of notes with instructions to take the money and travel to Rakhakapur, Gitapur and Akkalkot. On the direction of the hermit, he took the money and prostrated before him. The hermit and Sainath embraced each other and then walked outside just as they had entered through the door. The hermit told him to start the journey the next day and disappeared.

Early in the morning, the yogi went to the Gurusthan, the tomb (samadhi), Dwarikamayee and then went to Chavadi. He remembered the experience of the last night in Chavadi. He did not give much importance to the last night's incident as he thought it as a spiritual matter. He moved from Shiridi to Ganagapur and Nara Sobada where Swami Narasimha Sharaswati had spent most of his time. Swami Narasimha Sharaswati is also known as the incarnation of Dattatreya. Then he went to the tomb of Akkalkot Maharaj. Akkalkot Maharaj is also known as "Swami Samartha" and his words are received with respect by the devotees. He left his worldly body in 1878 CE. Some people even call him "Batabrukhya (banyan tree) Maharaj", because most of his time is spent under the banyan tree. He used to wear a dhoti and lived among the people of Akkalkot. Many kings and emperors were his disciples.

Hear I am writing something about Dattatreya which will help the Sai devotees to understand him. Dattatreya is Brahma, the creator, Vishnu the sustainer and Yogi Deva Deva Mahadev. The manifestation of all these is the appearance of Duttatreya. Duttatreya is a guardian deity who is not bound by any human Laws, not even by religious rules in this world and moves freely like the wind. In the same way, he gives protection to the people who possess the divine spirit. These great sprits (mahatmas) are called Abdhutas. Some of them live their life in naked state. They are known as Digambar Abdhutas. Their theories and practices are recorded.

SHRIGURU BHAGABAT : REVIVAL OF GURU TATTVA

The guidance and blessings of a Guru are inevitable in every worldly education and practice. Similarly, Guru is necessary to understand the perception or God's existence. The method of knowing God is known to the Guru and he will guide us. It is said in the scripture "Mantramulam Gurorbakyam, Mokhyamulam Guroh krupa". Veda - Vedant may be a treasure of knowledge. But all these are qualitative. The Guru is "transcendent and selfless" (Bhabatita, Gunatita). The Guru is above Ved-Vedant. A seeker who has firm faith in the Guru's words does not require anything else.

GURU TATTVA

God is a matter of self realisation, who should be experienced in a anxiety free state (Na kinchadapi Chintayagita - 6/25). As God is formless, Guru is with a physical form (Gopya). As He is Compassionate to us, he graces us through a medium i.e. physical body (Agopya). We unknowingly worship a body, a photo as our Guru. However, till then physically, a Guru has to be found. But this should be realised - Guru is not the body. Power of Guru (Guru shakti) or centre of Guru (Guru Kendra) is manifested by taking refuge in the body. The omniscient God pervades the inner soul of all Guru-kendras. Just as the power of God is imagined in any idol, so the mercy and control of God is to be seen in the Guru. Guru-kendra will be flourished based on the merit and potential of the disciple. Therefore, even if different people have different Gurus the Seed Mantra, meditation and praise of the Guru are the same. From this point of view, no matter who is the Guru, the disciple's firm faith and devotion is the main factor. When the discipleship is achieved, all sadhanas can be accomplished even through the clay idols of the Guru like Ekalabya.

As per the Scripture

Guraumanusyata Buddhih Sisyanam jadi Jayate,
Nahi tasya vabet Siddhih kalpakoti shaterapi.

If a person treats his Guru as a human being, even if he chants the God's name hundreds of millions years, then he will not achieve siddhi (enlightenment). God is eternal. He is all- Powerful, all - Pervading and all Controlling. Guru shakti is the active power of God.

Gurormadhye sthitam Bishwam,
Bishwa madhye sthito Guru.
Gurubishwam Namastestu,
Bishwagurum Namamyaham.

This universe is beyond the imagination of humans. To consider the Guru-shakti equally with the universe is not possible within the purview of the disciple's knowledge. From this point of view, it is written in the scriptures to meditate on the Guru.

Shwetambar shwetabilepyu ktam,
Muktaphalabhusitdibya murtim.
Bamanga pithe sthita dibyashaktim,
Mandismtitam Purnakrupa nidhanam.
Anandamananda karam, Prasannam
Sachhidmukhabhistam, baram pradan.

Jogindra Mitdyam Bhabarogabaidyam,
Shrimd Parambrahma Gurum namami.

Guru is the link between the world and God. It is mentioned in Gita that whose study of self realisation is very strong, whose mind is fixed on God, one who has a mind full of yoga, is free from any wants, is satisfied, is absorbed in the joy of God, sees action in inaction and inaction in action, whose actions are without any desires and intentions, free from attachment, eternally satisfied, void of envy, free from joy, grief and conflict, equal to success and failure wise, principled, whose all works have been burnt in the fire of wisdom, who has conquered the heart and the senses by abandoning all material pleasures – He is the Guru himself.

Tadbiddhi Pranipaten Pariprashnen Sebaya
Upadikhyanti te Gyanam Gyaninastatwa darshinah.

By going to such learned sages, prostrating, serving and questioning sincerely and simply one gets advice from this sage mahatma by which the life becomes successful and fruitful. Such mahatmas are the incarnation of God, established as Gurus and dedicated to liberate all from this worldly existences.

The meaning of Guru is not only a man with tatwagyan but Guru means knowledge and revelation. He, who destroys the darkness of ignorance and shows the light of wisdom and truth, is the Guru.

Gukarah Prathamo Barna mayadi Guna bhasakah
Rukar dwitiya Brahma maya vranti bimochakah.

The letter "Gu" means mayabi Guna (quality of illusion etc.) and "ru" means Brahma, the liberator of illusions. The word "Guru" is representing two forms i.e. Sagun (with form) and nirgun (without form). The wisdom which shows the changeability, impermanence and varieties of qualities of the world through constant change is Guru. The self realised person is Guru and the person who helps for self realisation is also Guru. Guru is the image of the soul – "Atma bai Gururek".

Mahapurus Atibadi Jagannath Das has written,

" the letter 'Gu' is above the virtue, formless is letter 'Ru' where these two qualities exist, he is called Guru".

The position of Guru in Indian culture is very high. Guru is described as possessing the power of creation, existence and destruction like Brahma, Vishnu and Maheswar. Gurushakti is prayed as a symbol of Parambrahma. This pure and clean Guru-disciple tradition of our country is mentioned in detail in the "Manu Smruti". The glorification of the Guru, the method of obeisance to the Guru, respect to the elders like Guru, the disciples behaviour towards the Guru's family, social behaviour towards Guru, the disciple's character and disciplined life, the merit of the disciple, the purpose and extent of acquiring knowledge, the preservation of knowledge etc. are reflected in Manusmruti.

It is told that-

Jatha khanan khanitrena naro barjyadhigachchati.
Tatha gurugatam bidyam shushrusuradhigachchati. (2/218)

Just as a man digs soil in a spade and finds water, so the sincere devotion, service and faith of the disciple is the ideal sacrificial fee for the Guru. God appears in the form of Guru for the welfare of the disciple. Guru is the supreme concept of God. A person with a body can only imagine God as a physical body, but a disciple by his service to the body of the Guru can get it as the holy and blessed body. But when the disciple enters in to the Brahma theory (Brahma - Tattva), the self-theory (Atma Tattva) – there remains neither the Guru nor the disciple. The enlightenment of the awareness of divinity, the awareness of self are to be felt by everyone but it is limited only in the realm of mind. There will be non duality (Adaitya) in the thinking process, but not in the action. Again, even if the thought of non duality (Adaitya Bhaba) is everywhere in the three world's (Swarga, Martya, Patala), it should not be with the Guru. Guru-disciple are dual (Daitya).

Till now, we understand -God and Guru are one. There is no difference between these two. But there is one. If the lord is pleased, then he will grant boon according to the desire of the devotee, whether the devotee asks for good or bad. The boy Dhruba wandered into the forest in search of God. Devarshi Narada appeared as his Guru and showed him the way to attain God. Sriman Narayan emerged and asked Dhurv for boons. Dhruv said "I do not need any boon at present. I was looking for glass but found gems. Now the glass is no longer required". God said "No. – It cannot be. You did not do penance to get me. You did penance to get a bigger kingdom than your father. That boon is to be taken now and enjoyed in this birth only." In this regard, God gives you what you need. Guru does not do like that. The Guru gives the disciple that which is beneficial to him. Even if the disciple does not want it, the guru gives him, which is good for him. From this point to view, in many cases the Guru is given a place above God.

It is said that -

Guruh pita gururmata gururdeb Gururgati
Shibe ruste guru swata gurou ruste na kashhan.

Guru is father, mother, god and the only mode of life. The Guru can save if Shiva is angry, but nobody can save if the Guru is angry.

Proof of this matter is available in "Sri Rama Charit Manas" in the context of kaka bhusandi. In one of the previous births, kakabhusandi was doing penance by chanting the name of Shiva. At this time his Guru entered there. In a defiant mentality, kakabhusandi did not get up and bow to the Guru. This does not make the Guru sad or angry. But Shivji could not bear the disobedience of the Guru. Shivii cursed Bhusandi through akashbani (voice from the sky). In this situation the benefactor Guru appeased Lord Shiv by praying and freed the disciple from the curse. This is the greatness of the Guru.

We address the Guru as "Baba" with respect. This word has a strange hypnotic power, creating a divine relationship between Guru-disciple and father- child. The vibration of this utterance is very sweet, blissful and soulful. The root of the word "Baba" is 'ba' which refers to cyclical, solitary and one after the other. The meaning of 'ba' in two applications (1) This otherwise that (2) This or that. In the first application, this may be different from that, but in the second application, this and that are the same. From the spiritual point of view God is the periodical order of the world. If you are worldly oriented, there will be obstacles in attaining God and if you seek God there will be slowing down in worldly activities. Therefore, through the first 'ba', man must decide, who is great, the world or God. If God is greater for him, then he will explore the second 'ba'. The second 'ba' is the Sri Guru, the periodical order of God himself. That means two 'bas' i.e. Baba is one who must renounce the world to progress towards attainment of God and to attain God one should realise the Guru Tattva. But giving up the family and directing the mind towards God is a very difficult matter. The reason for this is, God is infinite but man is finite. It is extremely difficult to find the infinite within the finite. The Guru is the finite form of the infinite and to reach the infinite, the finite medium is "baba".

Before finding and understanding the Guru, there is a necessity to inspire discipleship in the disciple. Who is called a disciple? The answer to this is "shisyastu ko jo Gurubhakta ebm" – who is a devotee of the Guru is the disciple.

One does not become a disciple through hymns (mantra) by taking initiation. The disciple should be devoted to the Guru. Anything other than the words of Guru should be understood as lies. Now it is day. If the Guru says that it is now night, the disciple should accept that with great faith. In the Guru there should come a sense of attachment. Guru is my God, soul, my own soul, dearest of all friends, most loving, most blissful than any one, most kin, most intimate – should be thought. Until the values of God is fully established in the human image of the Guru, one is not considered to have attained the Guru. Discipleship requires frequent discussions and analysis of the scriptures.

It is said in Srimad Bhagabat "Snigdhasya Shisyasa". Who is mature – pleasing is the one eligible to become a disciple. As rice becomes soft when cooked, so should the disciple be matured. Under no circumstances should a disciple withdraw. Unless a disciple is soft like this, he cannot grasp the knowledge of the Guru. Therefore, the Guru does not impart knowledge if the disciple is not matured enough.

In the Bhagabat Gita, Arjun says very restlessly,

"Shisyasteham shadi mam twam prapannam" (2/7).
Meaning – I am your disciple and refuge. Please teach me.

The discipleship of Arjun deeply touched the heart of Lord Srikrishna. Through Arjun, he has opened all the treasures of knowledge of Gita to the whole world.

The man is ignorant. He has no right to choose his spiritual path. This is proved by the scriptures, because he is ignorant of this. Guru is omniscient. He finds the best path for the disciple. Just as the doctor examine us, diagnoses us and prescribes medicine, so does the Guru prescribe the process of treatment for spiritual diseases. However, reaching near the Guru is the first step of the disciple. If you will go one step towards God (Guru), he will come forward ten steps towards you.

It is said in the Gita,

"Uddharedatatmanatmanam

Means – you should save yourself from the ocean of worldly botherations by yourself.

The saviour is the Guru, but we must make efforts to be saved. It is mentioned in the scriptures how a disciple should praise the Guru. In the first stage, when the disciple gets the vision of the true path, his eyes are opened, he realises the impermanence of the world – then he expresses his gratitude and prays to the Guru:

"Agyanatimirandhasya Gyananjanshatakaya

Chakhyurunnilitam jen tasmai shrigurube namah".

with the progress of penance, when he sees the Guru amidst the souls, then be will sing with joy:

Akhandamandalakaram byapta jena Characharam

Tatpadam darshitam jena tasmai shrigurube namah"

when the disciple perceives the Guru as Brahma, Vishnu and Maheswar or the Lords of creation, sustenance and destruction and in the form of the Lord Param brahma, prayers will automatically flow from the inner core of his heart:

"Gurubrahma Guruvishnu Gururdebo Maheswar Gurah sakhyat Parambrahma tasmat shrigurube namah"

In the extreme state of penance, when the disciple visualise the entire world filled with Braham, he experiences in a state in unchangeable bliss:

Brahmanandam Paramasukhadam kebalam Gyanamurtim, DwandatitamGaganasadrusham tatwamasyadilakhyam.
Ekam nitya bimalamachalam Sarbada Sakhibhutam, Bhabatitam trigunarahitam Sadgurum tam mamami.

From the proper presentation it is proved that even if, the Guru is one, the disciple will see various spiritual knowledges as per his condition. It seems appropriate to present here the dialogue between Hanuman and Sri Ramachandra in the Ramayan regarding penance. (sadhana)

One day Lord Shri Rama Chandra asked Hanuman affectionately "who are you, Hanuman." Hanuman was perturbed at such an unexpected question and said "Lord, I am your servant," God said nothing more and left with a soft smile. Many days passed. Hanuman remained engrossed in his penance. After some years, Shriram repeated the same question before Hanuman. But this time, Hanuman replied with confidence, "Lord, you and I are the same." This time too, without saying anything, the God left with a smile. Further much time passed. Hanuman entered from deep to deeper state of penance. Once again, Lord Shri Ramachandra asked "Hanuman, who are you?" But this time Hanuman answered gently "Lord, I am me, without me there is nothing in this world; this world is full of only me." This was probably the right answer to the question of God. God embraced Hanuman.

These three answers of Hanuman are the three conditions of a yogi. In the first stage, from the agility of the yogi's soul, the agility of the mind remains submissive. The Yogi's mind remains the slave of the soul. "Chanchalam hi manah krushna" (Gita 6/34). In the second stage, the yogi feels his soul and mind as God, which is the alternative samadhi in yogatattva of the yogis. In the third stage, the yogi becomes merged in "Nirvikalpa Samadhi" (a higher stage of awareness where the ego and sanskar have been dissolved and only consciousness remains) and feels the whole world full of the soul and self. This is a situation of self-realisation. These three answers of Hanuman are the three steps of entering into spirituality.

The Urdu poet has presented the three feelings of life in a very emotional way. e.g.

DAITYA BHABA (Duality)

"Gulsan me jake har Gulko dekha
Na teri rangat na teri bu hai."

Meaning – Gone to the garden and all the flowers I have seen
neither your colour nor your smell have been.

ADAITYA BHABA (Non duality)

"Gulsan me jake har Gulko dekha
Teri hi rangat teri hi bu hai."

Meaning – Gone to the garden and see all the flowers
only your colour and your smell remains.

ATMASTHA BHADA

> "Gulsan me jake har gulko dekha
> meri hi rangat meri hi bu hai".

Meaning – Gone to the garden and see all the flowers only my colour and my smell persists.

"SRIGURU BHAGABAT" is a great Guru tattva

The great "Guru tattva" (Principle of Guru) of ancient India and its meaning, must be grasped by every disciple. In fact, over the time, we have moved away from this great philosophy. In the kalki puran, all the future facts of Kali Yuga are presented. It has been said: the pollution level of religious propaganda and expansion will reach the extreme limit in kali yuga. There will be a strange deficiencies in the conduct of religion and the religion will become propaganda oriented. Without any background of their own penance, the persons dressed like saints (Sadhu panchakah) will emerge bearing the banner (Dharmadhwajinah) of dharma. The ascetics will immorally lead a secret worldly life (sanyasinau Gruhasakta). The cheats will become monks and live in the monasteries (Shatha mathanibasinah). The general household people who are qualified and entitled to take the responsibility of the society will be devoid of judgement and busy with their own work (Gruhasthasa – twabibekinah). If you will bath in the water of a holy place, you will get rid of all your sins and you will become righteous. In this judgement the people will arrange fairs and festivals to gather together (Dure nire tirthata). Religious books, music, sermons (in cassette form) will be sold in the market. People will earn a living through discourse. The religion will be traded in the market like a commodity. By acquiring it, people will gain self-satisfaction.

The disciples will blame the Guru who guides them in spiritual path, directly and indirectly (Gurunindapara). Otherwise, the teaching community (Guru kula) will be ignored and humiliated. At the government level, the education department will be neglected as a non-productive department. Among the problems of lack of teachers, lack of books etc. the employment of rental teachers will create a shameful situation in the education sector.

During such a confusing crisis, Pujya Guruji Shri Chandra Bhanu Satpathy Sir's "Sriguru Bhagabat" made an unique contribution. Such a comprehensive treatise on "Guru tattva" is rare in spiritual literature. The entire text is divided in to five parts. In this Shri Sadguru, definition of Guru, transition from ordinary human to Guru, types of Guru, devotees of Sriguru, types of devotees, Guru-disciple worship together, dikshadan by Guru and different levels and powers of diksha, Shri Guru life history, Shri Guru's body divinity, Sri Guru's supernatural powers, Shri Guru - disciple relationship, Guidance to Sadhaks by Guru, dhrama, death science, Karma and fruits of Karma, Guru Sadhana, Yoga Sadhana, attainment of God, worship to Guru, the method of Guru worship, Shakti-Siddhi-Bivuti, Penance, important subjects like Brahma and universe, blind faith, Curses and blessings, the divine relationships of some Guru - disciples, reaction to the first meeting with Guru, Siddhi - Tattva, grahasthya Dharma and Kala tattva etc. are described in detail.

Just as Shri Jagannath Das's Bhagabat written in nine letter verses, Shri Guru Bhagabat is composed in the same style. The language is very simple, easy to read and emotional. This book is a great medium for reviving the Guru-disciple tradition which is declining day by day in the society. It is certain that God's compassionate and controlling Guru shakti flows through Shriman Satpathy Sir as a fountain of devotion and inspiration. I thank my student Dr. Satchidananda Padhi for helping me in the analysis of Guru tattva, may God bless his family.

Supporting texts.

(1) Shrunwantu Amrutasya Putrah – Complied, edited by Shri Padmakanta Thakur "Bhagaban" (Based on Amrut Bachan of Shri Pujyapad Yogi – Guru Jwalaprad Tiwari ji Maharaj) – Publisher – Shri Sachchin Shankar Thakur, 231-15, Pataliputra Colony, Patna- 800013, Bihar (1996)

(2) Baidika Tathyara Baigyanik Bislesan (2nd and 3rd Part) – Dr. Satchidananda Padhi– Publisher – Odisha State Bureau of Text Book Production and Publication, Pustak Bhavan, Bhubaneswar (2009, 2011)

(3) Srimad Bhagabat Gita – Jagannath Das - Sanyasi Pustakalaya, Berhampur (2010)

GURUJI SHRI CHANDRA BHANU SATPATHY HAS EXPRESSED SOME OF THE FOLLOWING IDEALISTIC IDEAS: THOSE ARE –

Are you on the right path?

Please think on the matter written below again and again.

1. Why do you go to the temple of Shiridi Sai Baba? Because–

   (A) Do you love Baba so much that his momentary absence would make your like meaningless?

   (B) Would you like to take some time out of your busy schedule to pray, chant and worship at Baba's temple to awaken a healthy and pure state of mind?

   (C) Do you go to Baba's temple for blessings as you could not solve many problems around you?

   (D) Do you want to solve all your problems by Baba's grace within the specified time frame and by desired method?

2. Probably you have remembered, Baba has said that it is not inevitable for every seed to become a tree. Like that you may not get the desired result even if you come to Baba's temple. Will you believe it?

3. Do you ensure that what you offer to Baba is from your honest income?
4. Is it correct to gift Baba from the dishonestly earned wealth? What is your opinion?
5. Please remember how Baba had rejected the gold and silver gifts offered by the queen who came in a palanquin but accepted the bread and onion offered by an old woman.
6. Do you go to the temple to satisfy your feelings when your family and dependants are in trouble? Please remember, how Baba forced Mhalspathy who lived most of the time in Dwarakamayi to go back to his home and family.
7. Do you go to the temple for the company of others? Because you know a lot of people and find the temple a perfect place for unnecessary chatting with them. Is not it a useless waste of time to talk about Baba inside the temple?
8. Have you ever thought that the real good use of time is meditating on Baba, praying and participating in Arati or reading the books like Shri Sai Satcharitra etc.?
9. Is it right to talk unnecessarily about the fault of others, while none of us are perfect? It may be recalled here that Baba once told a man in the temple that how many people love to discuss the faults and weaknesses of others like pigs eat dirt.
10. Do you criticise other people's way of worship, because you think that your level of worship or devotion is much higher than others?

11. According to Baba, we face a lot of problems due to the rananubandh (refers to body's memory, which comprises of genetic memory and memory of intimate physical connect) of previous births. Do you agree with it ? If we believe in this, why not face our own problems instead of always crying or sulking?

12. Have you ever envisaged how much faith and tolerance do you have for Baba's presence? Is your faith variable with different issues and circumstances or is it always fixed and constant ?

13. Baba always advised on the following matters. They are kindness, non-prejudice, empathy, tolerance and self sacrifice. Have you ever sacrificed for others? Is what little sacrifices you have done enough?

14. According to Baba, when two people are fighting, the person who does not hurt the other or bear the blows of the other, is the most beloved of Baba. Do you do that?

15. Have you ever wondered, the uncontrollable emotions such as crying and screaming etc. are guides on the Spiritual path? By doing this, at times, you are harming others and polluting the good atmosphere. Is it not desirable to keep one's devotion to himself without making it public?

16. You always want everyone to sympathies with you and know you. Have you ever thought that other people also expect the same thing from you? Do you do like that?

17. Do you gain anything in devotional sphere by being jealous of other's progress ?

18. Whatever work you are doing for Baba, are they done with goodwill and full of devotion or just at random?
19. We always want Sai to solve all our problems. But have we ever tried to do some part of Sai's work in full ?
20. Do you want that God's blessings will come to you automatically, breaking all the karmik rules, whether you are eligible or not?
21. Should we not expect the blessings of Baba only after doing all his work? If you want Baba's blessings and want to live in peace with others, then it is your first and foremost duty to improve your qualifications by studying the above mentioned matters very well.

Think, Think and think

"Satpathy"

For the knowledge of the Odia devotees of Sai Baba:

Professor B.N. Mishra (Berhampur) has translated the original English writing in to Odia Language.

CHANAKYA NITI

Some of the under noted principles should be realised by all and should be guided accordingly.

Perhaps no other person in the history of India acquired as much knowledge in economics, science of war and astrology as Chanakya. His written principles are instructive and heartwarming, no doubt about it. The meaning of each sloka written by him is heart touching and applicable to people from all walks of life.

The meaning of the following verses are given in English.

1) "Kalah pachati bhutani Kalah Sanhaste Prajah.
Kalah suptesu jagarti kalo hi duratikramah"

The time swallows everything and destroys the creation. Time is also awake when all beings are in deep sleep. No one can resist the march of time. That means, time is so powerful that it is impossible to control it. There is description of time in Gita (Bhagabat Gita 10/30, 33, 11/37).

2) "Swayam karma karotyatma Swayam tat Phala mashnute
Swayam Bhramati Sansare Swayam tasmad mukhyate"

A man does his own work himself and he reaps the fruits of it. It is he who involves himself in the world and he is also freed from the cycle of birth and death i.e. attains Mokhya.

3) "Ananta sastram bahulantha
bidya alpascha kalo bahubighnatach.
Yat Sarabhutam Chadupasaniyam,
haso jata khira mibambu Madhyat."

Although there are many scriptures, many knowledges in this world, man cannot make full use of all the scriptures as his life span is short lived. One should try to use the selected scriptures as a goose takes only milk from the water mixed milk.

4) "Kah kalah kani mitrani ko desah koubyayaga moh kasyaham ka cha me shakti riti chintyam murhu murhu"

What to do at what time? Who are friends? What kind of place? How much income and how much expenditure? What am I? How much energy do I have? One should always ask himself these questions, so that he gets the answers to all the questions.

5) "Arthanasham manastapam gruhini charitanich
nichabakya chapamanam mahimanna prakashayet"

Loss of one's wealth, resentment for some reason, suspicious of wife's character and rude behaviour by some petty person, all these incidents should be kept secret without disclosing to anybody.

6) "Manasa chintatim karjya bwacha naiba Prakashayet
Mantrena rakhyayet gudham karya chapi neyejayet"

One should not reveal his planned thoughts to any one at all. This thought should be remembered as a Mantra. This mantra should be used secretly.

7) "Jo dhrubani parityajya adhrubam parisebate
   Dhrubani tasya nashyanti hyadhrubam nasta debahi"

The person who abandons certainty and runs after illusion will also not get certainty. The uncertainty is destroyed automatically. In the end, that person is left with nothing.

8) Murkhastu parihartabyah pratyakhyo dwapadah pasuh
   Bhinabhi bakya shatyen adrusham kasta koyatha"

One should stay away from fools, as if they are bipedal animals. This beastly man treats his ignorant speech like pricking with an invisible thorn. That means, a speech given by a foolish person without using his common sense is felt like the piercing of a thorn.

PROPAGATION AND EXPANSION OF SAI LEELA IN DIFFERENT COUNTRIES

The Shri Shiridi Sai institute of New Zealand started in 2002 and has grown into a huge institution for the glory and messages of Shri Shiridi Sai Baba. This institution has been established on a special spiritual mission, fulfilling the dreams of Auckland's urban devotees. The devotees of Shri Sai are doing Bhajans and prayer's every day and also every Thursday. The members of this institution, founded in the name of Shri Sai, have taken up programmes like blood donation camps, planting of saplings and food distribution. Under the supervision to Guruji Shri Chandra Bhanu Satpathy, a beautiful temple of Shiridi Sai Baba was built at Wahanga in Auckland. The temple is situated at 12-18, Princes Street, Wahanga, a city with a population of sixty lakhs and jointly funded by more than twelve hundred devotees. Many side deities – Shrishivling, Shri Ganesh, Shri-Ram, Shribalaji, Goddess Durga, Lord Hanuman, Lord Duttatreya and Navagrahas are also worshiped in this huge temple.

A huge hall for eating prasad and gathering has also been constructed in the temple premises. A special puja was performed here from 6th to 9th February in which about six thousand people gathered including devotees from various parts of the world like Chikago, London, Melbourne, Brisbane, Sydney, Hyderabad, Tirupati etc. Guruji Shri Chandra Bhanu Satpathy had participated in the function of the consecration of Shri Sai Vigraha's soul and the inauguration of the temple. On 9th February the souls of different deities were invoked and established in their respective vigrahs along with kumbhabhiseka or worship of kalas. A cultural extravaganza organised in the evening featured music composed by Guruji Shri Satpathy like Tubhyam Namami, Sriman Narayan Sai etc. The international Launch of the new book "The age of Shiridi Sai" written by Guruji Shri Chandra Bhanu Satpathy was also held.

The visit of Guruji to the Sanatan Dharma Temple and Cultural Centre in Kent (USA)

The arrival of Guruji Dr. Chandra Bhanu Satpathy at the Sanatan Dharma Temple and Cultural Centre in Kent (USA) on March 15, 2004 created joy and excitement amongst disciples.

Guruji eloquently explained to the assembled devotees in the temple court yard, the importance and predominance of the Guru in Hindu culture through the ages, saying that the Guru is the only means for the devotees to attain the divine goal through spiritual path. The arrival of Sadgurus on this world in different time period has always been resisted by contemporary prejudices and superstitions. Many Gurus appear from the most ordinary back grounds and deliver messages of Love and grace. Sadguru Sainath came from such a common background, led a very simple life. People of all religions, whether male or female, were blessed with his presence. In his company, the poor and the emperor received the same kind of hospitality. Further

Guruji said that the temples are primarily meant for devotees who go there to find peace and stability. But it may not be true that many times the management of the temple and the priests are jealous of each other and create disturbances. Guruji emphasized the responsibility of designated persons or centres for public relations and the co-operation of the voluntary forces. Guruji advised the devotees, desirous for the grace of Sadguru Sainath, to be of simple and saintly nature. If you want to offer something to Sainath, you should offer it very humbly and discreetly.

Do not discriminate and take any burden on yourself e.g. I am a generous man, I am a subscriber, I am a rich man, I am very poor, I belong to higher caste, I belong to oppressed class, I am a man, I am an woman, I am educated or I am illiterate. So that, the burden of such feelings does not rest on you. Do not go to Baba in fear or to show others but you go directly to Sairam for shelter at his feet. Do whatever you can in the service of Sairam. You can clean the floor, cook, tie flowers for Sairam or do any other work like this.

The true personality of Guruji was revealed when he answered a question from a devotee – "Please do not request me to bless you, I am an ordinary person like you. You pray for me. Only Sadguru Sainath can bless you".

After delivering the discourse, Guruji answered various questions of many devotees and prayed for their welfare. The volunteers of the "Sanatan Dharma Temple and Cultural Centre" danced with joy when Guruji said that he had come here as per the wish of the Lord or to fulfill certain specific purpose of the Lord.

The temple authorities expressed their gratitude to Guruji. Guruji surveyed the temple and its surroundings covering an area of about 15,000 square feet and made some suggestions for its further development.

Guruji Shri Chandra Bhanu Satpathy is revered in America

Born in the soil of Odisha, Guruji Dr. Chandra Bhanu Satpathy, who played an unique role in the propagation and expansion of the Sai movement in the world, has been honoured with the prestigious "Building Bridges across the nations" award for his outstanding contribution in the field of art, culture, music, Literature and above all humanity. Guruji was conferred with this honour in a grand ceremony held in Seattle, USA. It was a notable incident that the award was presented at a special event on the sidelines of the First Indo-US trade Summit. At first the citizens of Seattle had formally expressed their gratitude for spreading humanism through the teachings of Sadguru Shiridi Sai Baba, continuously in the world with love, kindness, tolerance and faith. After the announcement made by the Mayor of Seattle city, Lieutenant Governor Bread Owen had said that the splendid works performed in present times were of great importance. He hoped that Guruji would work to bring the Sai movement to every corner of America. Mr. N. Parthasarathi from Indian embassy and Mr. Brad Owen, the Lieutenant Governor of Washington State had taken part in the function as esteemed guest and chief guest respectively. While congratulating Guruji for this honour, Shri Parthasarathi observed that the activities implemented by him for the welfare of human Society is many times more than this award. At the end of the programme, dance programmes were performed by the artistes from various countries including India. While receiving the award, Guruji emphasized on using the culture, education and the need of the people to build the bridges of compassion, thereby reducing the distance between the countries. Many ministers and senior officials from different states of India had attended but none from Odisha. Governor of Washington State Mr. Kristen Gregory, Secretary of state Hilary Clinton, the Asia America Commercial Officer of white house Mrs. Kiran Ahuja and others had sent messages wishing success of the function.

Spirituality is the pursuit of Consciousness

On 28th January, Odisha Sahitya Academy organised a Programme related to "Literature and Philosophy" called "Srujan Sandhya" i.e. creative evening. This programme was held under the chairmanship of Srijukta Satakadi Hota, the President of Sahitya Academy. Attending it as the Chief Guest, Guruji Shri Chandra Bhanu Satpathy said that there are many ways to attain God. So, at first, it is necessary to know this road thoroughly. He, who unites his consciousness with a person's consciousness and takes it forward, is the Sadguru. He said that only a Sadguru can show a man the way to attain God. Similarly, going on to comment on Spiritual Literature Guruji said that it is based on egoless (Aham Shunya). Further he said that the thoughts generated inside oneself are the Spiritual Literature.

Spirituality is devotion and devotion is to Love God. Spirituality is man's search for his own consciousness. Philosophy, on the other hand, is meant for the development of Literature, is also the finest judge of principles. Guruji Shri Chandra Bhanu Satpathy told that all the saints are not literary Saints.

Shri Gaurang Charan Nayak, the honourable guest, said that spirituality is an improved part of the philosophy department. Just as the leaders of the spiritual world are different, the Literature of spirituality is also of different classes. Spirituality is not a work of any educational qualifications on any other achievements. There is no place for win or Loss. The achievement of a purpose may be the aim of the spirituality. Therefore, selfless service comes automatically to the mind of a man said Sri Nayak. On this occasion, Professor Narayan Satapathy (2010) and Late Dr. Kabi Prasad Mishra were felicitated by the Sahitya Academy. Shri Bijay Nayak, Secretary of Sahitya Academy, delivered the welcome speech and introduced the guests. Sri Rabi Ray gave thanks.

Book written by Shri Chandra Bhanu Satpathy, Launched Internationally

The book and music CD of Guruji Chandra Bhanu Satpathy were unveiled at a function organised by Shiridi Sai Temple in Seattle, USA. Guruji participated in this function and Launched the Hindi music CD "Baradan do Sai". Similarly, the English version of the third volume of Shri Guru Bhagabat was inaugurated here.

"Gopya ru Agopya" and its Sanskrit translation, unveiled by the Governor

Governor Shri Muralidhar Chandrakanta Bhandare on Monday released the Odia book "Gopya ru Agopya" written by Guruji Chandra Bhanu Satpathy and its Sanskrit version. "Srustitatwanu Chintanam" translated by Dr. Bhagirathi Nanda in an enchanting Literacy function. A large number of intellectuals and spiritual lovers from the State and outside the state attended the ceremony organised by Shri Shiridi Sai spiritual and Charitable Trust. In this speech Mr. Bhandare expressed, that the philanthropic and social welfare work of Odisha Shiridi Sai Trust is commendable. The Governor said that the Indian culture contains many signs of hidden knowledge in the Veda, Upanishads and various purans written in Sanskrit Language. They are not fully understood. However, the Governor hoped that the book of Guruji Shri Chandra Bhanu Satpathy would make many complex concepts simple and understandable. Guruji, the author of the book, said in his speech that every word used in Veda, Upanishad has a different meaning. The meaning of each word is broad, indicative and symbolic. Shri Satpathy explained his discourse with various examples. Many times people confuse spirituality with Science and try to prove Science superior. But it should be understood that, even within spirituality the principles, facts and philosophy of Science are in hidden state. He hoped that this book, written by him, would be able to answer many unanswered questions.

The grace of Baba will be obtained through undivided devotion: Guruji

The congregation of Shiridi Sai devotees have been held in Canberra and Sydney. Guruji Shri Chandra Bhanu Satpathy joined in the gathering and said that the blessings of Baba is obtained through undivided devotion. Every devotee should first be aware of his responsibility towards his family. He said that it would be a real service to Baba especially donating own Labor and helping any suffering being. In this gathering, Guruji enlightened on Shrimad Bhagabat and life cycle. Many devotees from Canberra and Sydney were present in this congregation.

Summary of Guruji Satpathy's address to Sai devotees at Bothel on 19.03.2014

On the 19th March 2014 at 7.30 PM, revered Guruji Shri Chandra Bhanu Satpathy-ji addressed about a hundred devotees of Baba in the Bothel (city in Washington State, USA) temple complex where Baba's Statue is being worshiped regularly along with that of some other deities. All the three groups of Baba's devotees of three cities were present. Later he performed the Sheja Arati, met people, had prasad and left about 9.30 pm.

Guruji Satpathy's visit to the Bothel temple was very nice and wonderful. The way he was telling casually about everything randomly – and at the same time very keenly answering questions in our hearts and minds. It was very wonderful to see how he read our hearts and responded to the unspoken wishes so immediately, just as the way Sai Baba used to answer devotees questions as a seemingly random talk.

An unforgettable evening in Australia in the company of Guruji Shri Chandra Bhanu Satpathy, the holy remembrance of Shri Shiridi Sai Baba

The month of February 2014 turned out to be a very memorable one for Sai's disciples living in Sydney and Canberra, Australia. On his return journey to India after inaugurating a temple of Shri Sainath in Auckland, New Zealand, Guruji's Shri Chandra Bhanu Satpathy was present in our gathering, performed Baba's bhajan and addressed us on His divine life history. Canberra is the capital of Australia and is a fully administrative state. The entire city falls silent after 6.30 pm. But on the eve of Shri Sai evening, the weary city was suddenly revived to hear the Spiritual Sermons from Guruji and receive his blessings.

I felt myself fortunate to have personally came in Contact with Guruji and received his blessing. The, devotees from Perth and Sydney came here to hear from the mouth of Guruji directly. This spiritual event was held on Wednesday, 12th February 2014, at 81, Ratcliffe Crescent floor, Canberra. Even in the middle of the busy week, people came continuously in large numbers to hear from Guruji. They were never disappointed, rather their thirst to know more about Shri Sai Baba was quenched when Guruji explained clearly, why he himself worshiped Sadguru Sai Baba. The gist of Guruji's speech was that it was futile to expect any miraculous benefits from Sai Baba because Baba was not a magician. The main thing is that a devotee should learn how to transform himself in to a good person. The rich and poor are equal in the eyes of Baba. Disapproving the casteism, boycotting of Leprosy patients from the Society, the mentality of neglecting the people in the Lower Strata in society and economy, he was giving messages to the people in the world by his daily behaviour. It was mentioned in Sai Sat- Charitra that Baba accepted an oppressed poor Leprosy patient named Bhagoji Sindhe as his lifelong servant. Once a child unfortunately stepped in to a burning furnace and got burned. Even though he was far away, Baba, knowing this, put his hand into the dhuni. His hand also got burnt. On asking, he said that the boy accidentally met with such an accident. I was saving him as his mother was calling me worriedly. Baba refused the doctors who wanted to treat his own burnt hand. Even when rich disciples came to apply ointment on his hand, Baba did not let them touch his hand. He was served only by Bhagosi Sindhe. Baba instructed that the food prepared from the pot should be distributed under one roof irrespective of the rich or poor. Baba was the divine symbol of mercy and grace, who treated everyone equally.

 Guruji faithfully advised that one should not bargain

with various deities and Sadgurus to fulfill his desires or to solve his problems. Guruji reiterated that human suffering is a natural phenomenon and life's ups and downs are also very natural. If one has strong faith in Sadguru then the disciple's problems are solved and the power of patience increases. The followers of Shiridi Sai Baba should experience and learn this characteristic of faith and patience. He also said that the disciples should not resort to falsehood to keep Sadguru on the top position. The devotees should not even participate in what is being transmitted about Sadguru's appearance in various places through TV and radio. Due to this, people get wrong idea about Baba. Baba disapproved of worshiping Him by neglecting his own family. Guruji said that for our spiritual ascension we should keep smaller goals than before and trying continuously to achieve them.

In response to a public question on how a common man can serve Baba, Guruji answered that anyone can spread the message of Baba by doing voluntary work at Shiridi Sai Baba's temple, publishing articles about Baba or opening a website to spread awareness among members of the trust or people. Further Guruji told that, all the time people requested him to talk about Baba. Expressing his gratitude to them, Guruji was overcome with emotion and said that he had benefited greatly by combining his thoughts with those of the seekers and remembering Baba.

Just after the discourse, Shej Arati started. Guruji led the gathering crowd by singing prayers himself. The children took the Chamar (A fan made of the bushy tail of the yak) from Guruji's hand and started fanning Baba. The temple way overflowed by the flow of the divine Stream. The tears of joy rolled down from everyone's eyes. One such spiritual gathering was organised on the 13th of February at the Shiridi Sai Baba temple in strathfield, Sydney with a large gathering.

The spiritual gatherings of many devotees in Canberra and Sydney showed that people, regardless of their caste and nationality, were not reluctant to pray with devotion and faith to Shiridi Sai Baba. The people thronged to know about Baba, mainly from the mouth of Guruji, because Shiridi Sai Baba always resides inside Guruji. The devotees were fortunate enough to view Sadguru and Govind at the same time in Guruji.

The joy of the people of Sydney and Canberra knew no bounds, no words to express it also. The two gatherings were concluded after taking Maha prasad. Pujya Guruji Shri Chandra Bhanu Satpathy graciously offered the Gems of holy name of Shirdi Sai Baba to the devotees of Canberra and Sydney which were received with reverence by all the devotees.

SOME MEANINGFUL AND SPIRITUAL ANALYSIS BY GURUJI SHRI CHANDRA BHANU SATPATHY (GOOD AND BAD SIGNS)

People believe God to be the greatest benefactor, most powerful, eternal and universal consciousness and His power can control the past, present and future of all the objects and creatures of the world. All philosophies and religions describe God as supreme, merciful and the source of all the happiness for the creatures of his creation. He is the statue of joy and the basis of eternal joy.

God is said to be omniscient, omnipresent and omnipotent and He is deified in all the world's religious scriptures, even in eastern and western metaphorical definitions. Except for the spiritually advanced persons and scholars, most devotees, while praying to God harbor a secret hope in their conscious and subconscious mind that they can gain God's mercy, support, help and self satisfaction through prayer. For them, happiness or contentment is the solution to life's mundane and psychological problems, which balances the minds of each individual.

A person who hopes to find a remedy for personal sufferings through prayer is not really a spiritual seeker. The seekers of God (Bhagabat Kamis) and true inquisitive devotees never wish that all the hopes in their life should be fulfilled and life should be full of happiness. Such persons experience so-called joy and sorrow equally, because they know that God's purpose and role in their experiencing the so-called joy and sorrow have equal consequences. God Almighty or universal nature through which God manages this creation, His plan is not that all creatures including human beings will be only good, then where does the creation of so-called evil come from ? If good is the opposite of evil, then there exists another powerful force which is equal to the power of benevolent God or an opposite existence who can enact only evil and we must acknowledge its presence. If we say that God is the only being who gives us the sense of good and evil, then it is impossible for any other power like "Satan" or sin to exist in the overall management of the world.

Hinduism talks about deities (Positive forces of the nature) and demons (negative forces of the nature). In Hindu mythology, demons and asurs, symbols of this negative energy, are said to collect energy from God. The fact that Brahma, Vishnu, Maheswar gave powers to the demons is sufficiently known from the purans. These negative forces or demons have specific roles in controlling the universe, like Light and dark, good and evil, these two forces are complementary to each other. One cannot exist without the other. Every good event or good deed has some evil in it. Similarly every bad event or deed has some good in it. Therefore, there is no such thing as pure good or pure evil.

The good and the evil are symbolised by gods and demons respectively. It is innate in human nature. When these two qualities of man interact with other human beings, then there is a clash of two opposing forces. They have shown and affirmed that there is no difference between their "Istadev" (Revered God) or God and Baba. So in the first stage of penance, the devotee first tries to see all deities within Baba's idol (Vigraha) and live life for Baba. In short in all scenes he should visualise only Baba. At first, it can be difficult. But with unwavering determination and faith he can achieve this. For that, keep up the efforts.

Birth - Death cycle and Salvation (Mokhya)

The Principle of Rebirth: The birth and death are two inviolable laws of human life. After birth, death is inevitable. In the flow of cosmic time, the human existence is as fleeting as water bubbles. The lives of billions of animals, including humans, are bound by the cycle of birth and death. These are all called living beings, although many of them are invisible to us. The scientific research has discovered the existence of many invisible creatures and even more species of animals are still remain unknown. We have no idea about their movements, activities, physical shapes. Their destruction takes place after a specific period. When a living being abandons its body, the five elements (earth, sky, fire, air, water) of it dissolve in nature.

What happens to the Living being after leaving the body? Does his soul exist? These questions come to the mind automatically. Some religions do not agree the rebirth after the death of a living being. According to the philosophy or some religions, the living being has to take birth again and again until complete liberation. This total liberation is called "Moksha" in Hinduism and "Nirvana" in Budhism. In view of this culture of rebirth, ancient Hindu sages have told us to abstain from vices from the childhood and to strive for good deeds.

Every action has an equal corresponding reaction. Newton's Law of motion proved this statement. Similarly Hindus believe that every action of a person has a consequence and he has to enjoy or suffer from it. But, the difference is that, in the human case the Karma (both good and bad) does not end in one birth, it continues from birth after birth. This doctrine of karma is describes in detail in Srimad Bhagavat Gita and other religious scriptures.

In order to get rid of this painful cycle of birth, i.e. to attain salvation (Moksha), Hinduism prescribed various ways to follow. Accordingly, some donate for the construction of the temple and some give food to the hungry, according to their ability. Some aspire to gain virtue (Punya) by going on pilgrimage. However, this aspiration of attainment is against the principle of Hinduism.

The present age is the era of entrepreneurship, the era of investing with a plan to make profit. If there is hope, desire in life, then it does not end the rebirth but prolongs the cycle of birth. Therefore, the selfless deeds (Niskama karm) are given more importance than all other deeds (karma). This reincarnation is also mentioned in Shri Sai Satcharitra and other texts related to Shri Shiridi Sai Baba. Baba informed several devotees about their previous births and their relationship with Baba in those births.

Baba clearly explained that this omnipresence of God can be realised through the study of Shri Sai Satcharitra and this is the best way to attain God. So Baba's devotees should think of Him as formless, abstract, incorporeal while worshiping Him. If an idol is at all required for concentration of mind then is the idol of Baba not enough?

KALATATTVA

(One of the thirty six tattvas, according to Saiva doctrine)

Abibhajya kala tattva – (The principle of indivisible time)

The classical definition of what we call time is kala or Mahakala. In scriptures or poetry, this kala is called mahakala, mahakali, kala Purus, kala raja etc. In Sikhism and other religious sects it is called "Akal".

Our past, present and future – all these are included in time (kala). The period of time from birth to death is called life span (Jivan kala). The state of incorporeal existence after a living being leaves the mortal body is called Preta kala.

This living being takes birth in the universe. Lives for some time. Enjoys the life. Right from the moment of birth, karma chakra or Prarabdha (Predestined) controls the course of his life. Not only the animal world, the world of plants but the entire sky is subject to this time. Billions of universes, stars, suns, milky-ways and constellations are born in the infinite void. And after the end of their journey they again disappear in to the void. The life span of Avatars, Saints and Sadgurus is predetermined.

The great power of Param brahma and the power of time were hidden in the golden egg (Hiranya anda). In a fraction of a millionth of a second, the golden egg (Hiranya anda) was exploded and from it emerged the Progenitor (Adi purus) (Primordial man). That primitive man who appeared in the bright light of Hiranya (Gold) was called Kala Purus (Divine cosmic being).

However, the process of explosion was not permanent.

This was the initial stage of evolution. Gradually, its sphere of shining began to spread. Innumerable animals appeared.

The time is very precious in human life. He is born as a human being due to the deeds (karma) acquired in previous births. He has got an opportunity to do benevolent deeds in his current life. Every year, every month, every day, every minute - even every Second has its importance. He who does not use his time meticulously, his cycle of birth will not be stopped. He has to take birth again and again in order to fulfill his karma.

If we study the lives of Jesus Christ, Adi Shankaracharya, Vivekananda etc., it is known that even though they lived for a shorter period, they achieved the ultimate goal of life. At the age of only fourteen, Shri Ram killed the mighty demons. Shrikrishna performed miraculous acts from the childhood. Even after living for a long time, many do not make spiritual progress. Shri Sainath was under the tutelage of his Guru, at the age of only five. He reached Shiridi at the age of only 17 or 18. By that time he had attained Brahmatwa.

The question of whether we are making the best use of our time following the path directed by Guru, should always be kept in mind. One, who is aware of this particular aspect, achieves all success in his life. One who is not able to utilise the time positively, should be suffering due to the deeds (karma) of his previous births. He is facing hurdles in achieving his aim. Everyone should remember this discourse of Shri Sai.

PRALAYA PRASANG

Human beings have unlimited power to deal with various adversities that occur daily in the natural and living world, whether voluntarily or under duress, he confronts stressful situations. This is his profession. Our ancestors weathered the ravages of earth quakes, floods, fires, deadly diseases and more for the millions of years, from the Paleolithic age till today. At that time, people had no idea about science and technology. Life was difficult and dangerous. He was tormented by hunger. He was constantly changing his habitat in fear of being attacked by wild animals. He considered each day as a gift from the God. God was not in his imagination. So he had no hope of getting protection from God. He was guided by the direction of the nature. Despite all this he existed, although the giant dinosaur species have become extinct over the time.

A mind's eye view of the long continuous events from the Paleolithic age to the age of science and technology gives us a clear picture of the status, struggle and new ventures of the human race, Space travels, genealogy, marine inventions, internet communications, cloning process, nuclear power are just a few examples of human achievements.

Currently, the balance of environment and nature is not maintained. We get enough examples of this from media and internet sources. This is a great warning to the entire human race.

However, this warning of nature or environment is not for the first time for him. Over the past four million years, the earth's climate has undergone many changes. Sometimes the snow currents are flowed and sometimes the temperature of the atmosphere has increased abnormally. Even without any scientific concept, the man has resisted this rain of snow and rain of fire by applying his innate intelligence and ingenuity. And today when science and technology have made unprecedented progress, then why is there such an baseless fear of disaster (Pralaya) ?

The Vedic saints of ancient India were well versed in astrology and astronomy. They had estimated the age of the creation by their foresight and calculation. According to them, the duration of creation is very long. All these fifteen-digit number yugas are divided in to Mahayuga, Kalpa, Manwantar. According to the oldest Hindu scripture of ancient astrology "Surya Sidhant" (solar theory), the Kali Yuga began on 14th February, 3102 BC and its duration is for 4,32,000 years. Now in the year 2013 AD, the age of Kali Yuga is 5115 years. If we take this calculation in to consideration, then how can we accept that the Kali Yuga will be destroyed soon and the Satya Yuga will be established ?

The strange and delusional prophecies, such as the occurrence of Pralaya and destruction of the creation at a certain point of time, on a certain day are published in many magazines. Hundreds of years ago some self centered, arrogant people / groups who declared themselves as the representatives of God gave such shocking, misleading information.

They can be forgiven for their ignorance. But even after the modern man has realised the wide range of science, how can he believe this? Not only does he believe, he frantically runs to temples and astrologers to find relief from the tyranny of the tragedy. If there is a real pralaya, then how will one survive when everyone is perished. We should think that the astrologers who are giving inauspicious information like Pralaya, why did not they forecast when and on which moment the man will land on the Lunar

Surface? Why were they silent about other creative, successful human endeavors?

I have been hearing many things about it since I was ten years old. Somewhere sacrificial and ceremonial rites (Jagya) are performed to avoid the impending disaster. Somewhere else, remedial measures are being taken to satisfy the wicked powers. I still observe, the people are getting excited by such ridiculous prophecies, thinking it to be true, and engaged in these works. Such a state of mind has pushed them in to a sphere of panic and confusion. The reasoning or realistic view of them have disappeared. A true devotee of Sadguru Sainath should not believe at all in such baseless things. If we pray to Sadguru, he will give us the appropriate answers to all our questions and fears. This is my firm belief.

May Shri Sai bless us all on the auspicious day of Guru Purnima.

BLACK EAGLE BOOKS

www.blackeaglebooks.org
info@blackeaglebooks.org

Black Eagle Books, an independent publisher, was founded as a nonprofit organization in April, 2019. It is our mission to connect and engage the Indian diaspora and the world at large with the best of works of world literature published on a collaborative platform, with special emphasis on foregrounding Contemporary Classics and New Writing.

www.ingramcontent.com/pod-product-compliance
Lightning Source LLC
Chambersburg PA
CBHW060602080526
44585CB00013B/653